W9-CAI-323

19499

VIETNAM
THERE AND HERE

Margot C. J. Mabie

VIETNAM
THERE AND HERE

Holt, Rinehart and Winston   *New York*

Published by Holt, Rinehart and Winston, 383 Madison
Avenue, New York, New York 10017.
Published simultaneously in Canada by Holt, Rinehart
and Winston of Canada, Limited.
Library of Congress Cataloging in Publication Data
Mabie, Margot C. J.
Vietnam there and here.
Bibliography: p.
Includes index.
Summary: Discusses the war in Vietnam, the turmoil it
caused in this country, and the issues it raised that still
remain a source of conflict.
1. Vietnamese Conflict, 1961–1975—Juvenile literature.
[1. Vietnamese Conflict, 1961–1975]   I. Title.
DS557.7.M32   1985   959.704'3   84-20518
ISBN: 0-03-072067-2

First Edition

Designed by Lucy Albanese
Map by David Lindroth
Printed in the United States of America
1   3   5   7   9   10   8   6   4   2

Photographs courtesy of Wide World Photos

ISBN 0-03-072067-2

Overleaf: U.S. paratroopers in South Vietnam

For my father,
VINCENT STARBUCK JONES

Contents

Preface   *ix*

PART I. The Field of Battle

1. Vietnamese Roots   *3*
2. West Comes East   *10*
3. The Nationalists   *17*
4. The Indochina War   *24*

PART II. Americans Take to the
        Field of Battle

5. The Geneva Accords   *33*
6. The Two Vietnams   *38*
7. The Insurgency Begins   *44*
8. The Coup   *52*

CONTENTS

PART III. The American War in Vietnam

9. President Johnson's War   61
10. Escalation   68
11. President Nixon's War   75
12. Negotiations   81

PART IV. The Vietnam War in America

13. The Hawks   91
14. The Doves   97
15. The Media   103
16. Protest at Home   110

PART V. After the Battle

17. The Communist Victory   119
18. Vets at Home   125
19. The Weakened Giant   131
20. Sorting It Out   136

Afterword   141

Glossary   143
Notes   147
Bibliography   154
Acknowledgments   158
Index   160

Preface

Vietnam.

Twenty-five years ago, many Americans had difficulty locating the country on a map. Today, many Americans have difficulty locating the war in their minds.

The Vietnam War was one of the most painful events in all of American history. In 1965, when the first American combat soldiers went to war in Vietnam, Americans went to war at home. Proponents of the war—called hawks—believed that the United States, born of the desire for liberty, cannot sit by when communism denies people their liberty. Opponents of the war—called doves—protested against the war for a variety of reasons. Some believed that Vietnam was torn by a revolution or a civil war and that it is not proper for the United States to meddle in the internal affairs of any country. Others believed the war was simply unwinnable.

When American troops finally came home, in 1973, they sometimes found themselves still embattled. Veterans were often vilified by both proponents and opponents of the war, who saw them either as agents of American defeat or as agents of

American immorality. In many cases the veterans were simply ignored. There were no heroes. Now, years after the war in Vietnam was ended, the war at home continues.

Many Americans have never come to a conclusion about the U.S. involvement in Vietnam. This seems strange, for never before had Americans at home been offered so much information about a war. Day after day, on television they saw footage of bombing runs, platoons moving slowly through jungles, body bags. In newspapers and magazines, they read heavily illustrated articles about corruption in the South Vietnamese government, the Tet Offensive, Vietcong assassinations. At the same time, the media were covering the war at home. Day after day, Americans saw and read about peace marches, draft dodgers, draft-card burnings. It was not long before many Americans came to regard protesters as the real enemy.

After the war, Americans still disagreed, but they did so in silence; Vietnam seemed almost a taboo subject. The renewal of discussion about the war is a sign of our health and our hope. It is clear that the Vietnam War will haunt us until we understand it. It is also clear that the United States will be a weakened giant until we develop a new sense of when and how we will wage war. Too young to have heard the debate while the war was raging in Vietnam, you now hear the debate that has revived at home. This book chronicles the war in Vietnam and the turmoil it caused at home, and outlines the larger issues involved in both. I leave to you, the reader, to decide if—and why—the war was right or wrong. You were not a part of the war in Vietnam, but you will be a part of the new debate at home.

PART I

The Field of Battle

All men are created equal. They are endowed by their Creator with certain inalienable rights, among these are Life, Liberty and the pursuit of Happiness.

—Ho Chi Minh,
Declaration of Independence
of the Democratic Republic
of Vietnam[1]

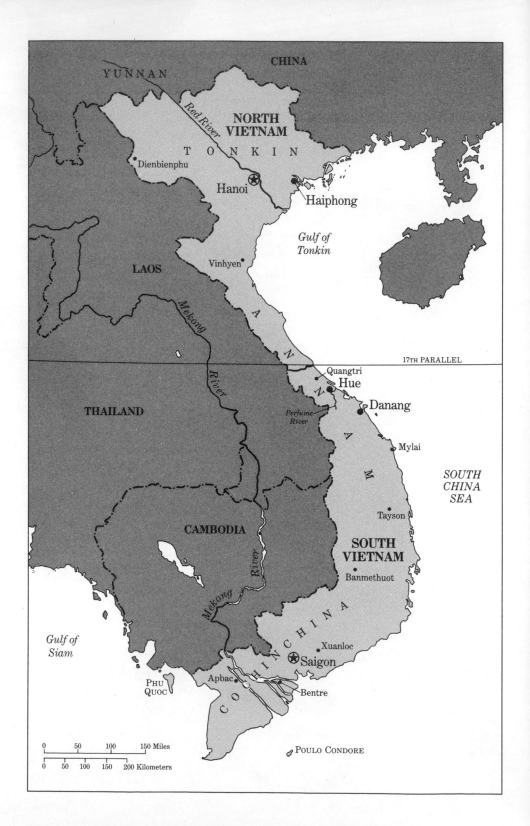

CHINA

YUNNAN

NORTH
VIETNAM

TONKIN

Red River

Dienbienphu

Hanoi

Haiphong

*Gulf of
Tonkin*

LAOS

Vinhyen

A
N
N
A
M

Mekong

River

17TH PARALLEL

THAILAND

Quangtri

Hue

*Perfume
River*

Danang

Mylai

SOUTH
CHINA
SEA

Tayson

CAMBODIA

Mekong

River

SOUTH
VIETNAM

Banmethuot

C
O
C
H
I
N
C
H
I
N
A

Xuanloc

Saigon

*Gulf of
Siam*

PHU
QUOC

Apbac

Bentre

0   50   100   150 Miles

0   50   100   150   200 Kilometers

POULO CONDORE

1

Vietnamese Roots

Vietnam today is an S-shaped country on the eastern edge of the large Asian land mass known as Indochina. The coastline, which extends more than 1,200 miles, is about as long as the Atlantic coastline of the United States from Maine to Georgia.

Despite the long border formed by the sea, the Vietnamese have always looked to the land for their livelihood. The country's two delta areas—the Red River delta, in the north, and the Mekong River delta, in the south—are astoundingly fertile. Blessed with unusually rich soil, plenty of water, and a tropical climate, the Vietnamese developed a society focused on the sowing, growing, and reaping of rice. Because of their country's shape and its primary crop, the Vietnamese frequently compare their country to two rice baskets at either end of a pole. The northern area of the country embracing the Red River delta, often called Tonkin, represents one basket. The southern area of the country embracing the Mekong River delta, often called Cochinchina, represents the other. The skinny corridor connecting the north and the south, often called Annam, represents the pole.

Today, Americans have a hard time envisioning Vietnam's shimmering rice paddies. Instead, we see only battlefields. Defeated there, we struggle to understand just what went wrong with our Vietnam War. To do so, we must go back to the beginning, for history is like a web, and the strands of the present were spun in the past.

According to one legend, the Vietnamese people trace their origins to the marriage of Lac Long Quan (pronounced Lock Long Kwahn), the Dragon Lord of Lac, and Au Co (pronounced Oh Kuh), the daughter of a Chinese emperor. When Au Co gave birth to a sack of eggs from which one hundred sons hatched, Lac Long Quan became unhappy with his wife. They parted, each with fifty sons. The father took his fifty sons south; the mother took her fifty sons north to a place near present-day Hanoi. Hong (pronounced just as it is spelled), the oldest of the boys in the north, started what became known as the Hong Bang dynasty, a succession of emperors from the same family line, which is said to have lasted from 2879 to 285 B.C.[2]

Many scholars believe that there was no such dynasty. Instead, they believe that during that period northern Vietnam contained only various unorganized tribes. But even if it is not true, the legend has a rich significance for the Vietnamese. Au Co's parentage accounts for the similarities between the Vietnamese and the Chinese. Lac Long Quan, with his dragon blood, fits in nicely with all the demons and spirits that the Vietnamese have always worshiped. The legend accurately locates the first state of Vietnam in the north. At the same time, it places people of a common ancestry in the south. Most important, the legend expresses a fierce sense of Vietnamese identity.

Scholars do agree about the arrival of the Chinese. In 208 B.C., Trieu Da, a Chinese warlord, marched south and conquered the peoples in the Red River delta. He then established his own kingdom, independent of China. He named it Nam Viet, which means Southern Country of the Viet. Less than a hundred

4

Vietnamese women with their age-old baskets, here used for salt

years later, in 111 B.C., the Chinese took control of the kingdom, renaming it Giao Chi.

Chinese rule lasted almost without a break for more than a thousand years. Chinese government officials, known as "mandarins," held the high positions. Vietnamese landowners, however, were permitted to manage their own land and all the people who lived and worked on it.

During their period of dominance, the Chinese brought to Vietnam many aspects of their culture that would endure long after they themselves were evicted. They brought the Chinese system of government, the Chinese writing system, which was adapted for the Vietnamese language, and the Chinese educational system. They also brought Buddhism, a religion developed in India. They introduced the use of water buffalo in agriculture and an intensive system of growing rice.

The Vietnamese accepted much of the Chinese way of life, but they refused to accept Chinese rule. The Chinese state demanded large sums of money from the Vietnamese landowners, which they in turn raised by taxing the peasants who lived on their land. In addition, the Chinese forced the Vietnamese to work for them, either serving in the Chinese military or providing labor for the many Chinese building projects—roads and canals and ports by which the Chinese could send home some of the enormous quantity of rice harvested in this land to the south. The harsh demands made by the Chinese and the remarkable sense of national identity among the Vietnamese gave rise to rebelliousness. Throughout the long Chinese occupation, Vietnam bubbled with unrest.

The Trung sisters, among the most revered patriots in Vietnamese lore, represent an example of this unrest. In A.D. 39, the Chinese governor of Vietnam assassinated a landowner. The governor intended to make the Vietnamese so fearful that they would cooperate. Instead, his act inflamed the landowner's widow, Trung Trac (pronounced Troong Trahk). She and her sister, Trung Nhi (Troong Knee), raised an army, which eventually overwhelmed the Chinese. For two years, the Trung sisters ruled as queens. But the Chinese wanted their colony back, and they fought to regain supremacy. Defeated in A.D. 43, the Trung sisters committed suicide by drowning themselves in a river.

After the Trung revolt, the Chinese held Vietnam in a tighter grip. Still, the Vietnamese continued to try to break Chinese rule. Finally, in A.D. 939, they succeeded. China was at that time ruled by the Tang dynasty, which had grown very weak. With disunity at home, China was unable to put down a revolt in Vietnam.

Except for a twenty-year period during the fifteenth century, Vietnam was from then on able to maintain its independence from China. The Vietnamese emperors kept their northern neighbor at bay by paying China an annual tribute. On occasion, the Vietnamese had to fight. Often outnumbered and poorly armed, they became masters of guerrilla-warfare techniques. The term *guerrilla war*, derived from the Spanish for "little war," refers to a conflict between a small, poorly equipped force and a large, well-equipped army. Outnumbered and outgunned, guerrillas tend to avoid classic battles in which both sides array themselves on the field. Their goal was to defeat the enemy by attrition—the process of wearing down. Vietnamese guerrillas made lightning-fast attacks on small groups of enemy soldiers far away from the enemy's main areas of control. Like mosquitoes, the guerrillas kept the Chinese troops rushing to swat one pest here, another there. When the enemy was tired and disorganized, the guerrillas attacked the main force.

China's army marched south and gained control of Vietnam one more time, in 1407. The inevitable rebellion was led by a landowner named Le Loi (pronounced Lay Loy). He raised an army and trained it in the guerrilla tactics that had already worked against the Chinese. The guerrillas began attacking the

Chinese troops posted in rural areas. As the attacks grew worse, the Chinese pulled farther and farther back until they were concentrated in the cities. Le Loi was then able to mobilize even more Vietnamese citizens. By 1427, the balance of power had shifted to the Vietnamese, and the Chinese were sent packing.

Le Loi became emperor, and he and his successors set out to organize and strengthen Vietnam. The government, fashioned after China's, was made effective and efficient; an army was developed; education and the arts were encouraged; a legal system was put in place; a land-reform program gave ownership of valuable rice paddies to the peasants.

The state of Vietnam also expanded. Originally confined to the north around the Red River delta, the Vietnamese had begun moving south in the tenth century A.D. A village would send some of its people south to set up a new village. The new village relied on the mother village until it was well established. Once established, the new village sent some of *its* people farther south to create yet another new village. Village by village, Vietnam grew to include the Mekong River and its lush delta.

As it grew far beyond its original boundaries, Vietnam was less and less under the control of its emperors in the north. Local landowners began vying among themselves for power. By the end of the sixteenth century, two families had emerged as the strongest forces in the country. The Nguyen (pronounced Win) family managed the south; the Trinh (Tring) family managed the north. Both families formally recognized the emperor as head of the nation, but, unable to contest their power, the emperor's rule was diminished. In the 1630s this split was given physical proof when the Nguyen family built two walls across the plain of Quangtri, in slender central Vietnam. The division was at once a haunting reminder of Vietnam's legendary past and an eerie foreshadowing of Vietnam's tragic future.

Despite the walls, the separation between north and south did not last. In 1772, three brothers from Tayson began a peasant rebellion against the wealthy ruling class. Starting in the south, the Tayson army defeated the Nguyens, then moved north to defeat the Trinhs. By 1787, all of Vietnam was again under the control of a single leader. But the Tayson army's rule failed to hold the loyalty of the people, and a member of the defeated Nguyen family would later rise to take the army's place. In the process, he whetted the colonial appetite of another foreign nation—this time, France.

2

West Comes East

Visitors from the Western world had been to Vietnam as early as A.D. 166, but not until the sixteenth century did Westerners come with the intention of staying. In 1535, the Portuguese established a trading station at Faifo, a harbor about fifteen miles south of present-day Danang. Other European traders, equally excited by the riches of the East, soon followed.

Along with commerce, the Portuguese were eager to spread Christianity, so Portugal sponsored Catholic missionaries in Asia. One of the first—and surely the most impressive—of the missionaries the Portuguese sent to Vietnam was a Frenchman by the name of Alexandre de Rhodes. He arrived in 1627 and quickly mastered the Vietnamese language. In addition to converting thousands of Vietnamese to Catholicism, he developed Quoc Ngu, a writing system for the Vietnamese language using the Roman alphabet.

The Vietnamese emperors were of two minds about what Rhodes and other missionaries might mean to their country. They were intrigued by the missionaries' knowledge but worried by their beliefs. The Vietnamese government, after all, was rooted in Confucianism, which focuses on the group rather than the individual. Developed in China, Confucianism is a moral system aimed at promoting the highest state of humanity. Family ties of respect and obedience are emphasized. Both the Chinese and Vietnamese governments were based on Confucianism, for as the child respects and works harmoniously with his family, the adult will respect and work harmoniously with the state. The emperors had always been leery of Buddhism, which holds that the individual must free himself from all worldly desires in order to attain nirvana—release from the Wheel of Life, and thus from suffering. But what about Christianity, which stresses the individual's relationship with God? Would Christian converts continue to give their loyalty to the emperor? Further, would the Westerners take over Vietnam if Christianity gained many converts?

Unsure about the missionaries, the Vietnamese emperors were sometimes helpful, sometimes hostile, to the priests. In 1630, Rhodes himself had to flee the country. However, he was still convinced that Vietnam was fertile ground for the Catholic church. He returned to Europe to get backing for a vigorous missionary effort. Because Portugal was by then a weakened power, Rhodes turned to his native France for support. To make his proposal irresistible, he described Vietnam as a country rich in both religious and commercial possibilities. His efforts in France succeeded. In 1664, the Society of Foreign Missions was established. Its goal was to spread Catholicism in Asia and to assist French businessmen to develop trade.

Both priests and traders found work in Vietnam difficult. Many of the Vietnamese people did not like foreigners, and they could be roused to fight them. When the Vietnamese were not fighting with the foreigners, they were often fighting among themselves, making the country unsafe even for outsiders. As a result, Dutch, English, and French traders left Vietnam to concentrate their efforts in other areas of Asia.

The missionaries, however, did not give up so easily. Pierre Joseph Georges Pigneau de Béhaine was sent to Vietnam by the Society of Foreign Missions in 1767. Ten years later, he found himself in the midst of the Tayson rebellion. When the rebels overwhelmed the Nguyen family, who controlled the south, they massacred all of the Nguyens they could find. One member of the family who survived was Nguyen Anh (pronounced Win Ong), then a sixteen-year-old boy. With the help of Pigneau, he escaped to Phu Quoc, an island in the Gulf of Siam. From there, Nguyen Anh attempted to reassert his family's rule.

In 1787, Pigneau took Nguyen Anh's cause to the French court of Louis XVI. The king had many problems with France itself, but Pigneau convinced Louis that France's rivals would get into Vietnam if he missed this opportunity. Louis XVI reluctantly agreed to assist Nguyen Anh. France would supply men, arms, and transport. In return, France would be given the city of Danang, Poulo Condore Island (off Vietnam's southwest coast), and exclusive commercial privileges. Louis later withdrew his support, but Pigneau took over the forces, paying them with funds raised by French businessmen in India, who were promised trading opportunities in Vietnam. For ten years, Nguyen Anh and his Vietnamese followers fought the Tayson rebels, finally defeating the last of them in 1801. In 1802, he crowned himself emperor, taking the name Gia Long (pronounced Jah Long).

The new emperor owed nothing to the French government, so Danang, Poulo Condore Island, and the exclusive commercial privileges offered by Nguyen Anh in 1787 were not given to France. But in appreciation for Pigneau's help, Gia Long permitted traders and missionaries to work in Vietnam. His successor, Minh Mang (pronounced Min Mahng), was not so tolerant. His instinctive fear of foreigners grew as revolts broke out, revolts he blamed—accurately—on the priests. Under Minh Mang, missionaries were executed, converts were persecuted, and trade was made not worth the effort for French businessmen.

A petty cab driver having his fortune told

Four decades after Nguyen Anh became Emperor Gia Long, the French government and French businessmen felt renewed interest in Asia. Other countries were gaining access to Asian goods, and France wanted a part of the action. The difficulties the missionaries and their converts were encountering in Vietnam now served as a good excuse for French intervention.

In 1844, ten years after his arrival as a missionary in Vietnam, Dominique Lefèbvre joined other priests who were plotting to replace Emperor Thieu Tri (pronounced Tee-ow Tree) with an emperor who favored Christianity. Caught, Lefèbvre was to be executed. Thieu Tri reconsidered, and Lefèbvre was expelled from the country. Determined to work in Vietnam, Lefèbvre sneaked back in in 1847. Again he was caught, sentenced to death, and then deported.

In the meantime, a French naval squadron stationed in China had sailed for Vietnam to save Lefèbvre, though it arrived in Danang weeks after he had been deported. There a clash developed over a matter of protocol—the French had been spoiling for a fight. When the squadron set sail, much of the harbor had been destroyed, and many of the citizens of Danang had been killed. Angry, Thieu Tri and his successor, Tu Duc (pronounced Too Duck), tried to rid Vietnam of Christianity.

Increasing persecution of the troublesome missionaries became the excuse for France's increasing belligerence. But France's desire to maintain its national glory and acquire Asian possessions was at the root of its efforts there. In 1858, the French returned to take Danang. That done, they sailed to Saigon. Saigon did not fall as quickly as Danang. The French took the city after two weeks, but they could not claim real control until additional French forces arrived in 1861.

In the end, Emperor Tu Duc gave France three provinces around Saigon, Poulo Condore Island, and three ports. The French, in effect, had established a colony. The emperor also agreed that the missionaries could remain. Tu Duc had no alternatives. Faced with firm French control over the Mekong River delta area, he was also being challenged by Vietnamese rebels in the north. His one hope was that the French, unused to the Vietnamese climate, would wilt in the heat and fall victim to disease.

The French did not succumb to the Vietnamese climate. Nor were they satisfied for long with their limited holdings in Vietnam. In 1867, the French commander in Saigon seized three more provinces in the south. Not long after that, the French began eyeing the north.

Looking for a route to China, they explored the Mekong River, which wends its way from Yunnan Province, in southern China. But the river was in some areas unnavigable. However, the Red River, in the north, provided an ideal route. When the Vietnamese in Hanoi tried to prevent a French arms merchant, Jean Dupuis, from using the Red River to get to Yunnan, Dupuis rallied foreign businessmen in Hanoi, and in 1873 they occupied a section of the city. Dupuis then appealed to Admiral Jules-Marie Dupré, the French governor of Cochinchina, for troops to help hold Hanoi. Dupré was happy to oblige.

Back in Paris, the French government was disturbed when it learned that some of its citizens, on their own initiative, had raised the French flag over a part of Hanoi. In 1874, France signed a treaty with Emperor Tu Duc by which Dupuis and the French forces called in from Saigon were expelled from Tonkin, the name the French used to refer to northern Vietnam. In regaining sovereignty over Tonkin, Tu Duc confirmed France's colonial rights in all of the south—Cochinchina—granted transit on the Red River, permitted the French to set up three consulates in the north, and authorized the French to help defend Vietnam's border with China.

This last provision the French seized upon ten years later to take over all of Vietnam. Chinese bandits had been crossing the border into Vietnam and raiding rural villages. Ostensibly to end the raids, but in reality to gain control of the entire country, the French decided to make the rest of Vietnam a protectorate. (Unlike a colony, which is governed by a representative from the colonial power, a protectorate is governed by a native citizen, who is advised by a representative from the "protecting" power.) In 1883, the French fleet sailed to the mouth of the Perfume River and immediately began a siege. Overwhelmed by events and without a leader—Tu Duc had died a few months before without a successor—the mandarins were forced to give up the remainder of Vietnam to France.

Agreement in hand, the French took control, ruling the protectorate just like the colony of Cochinchina. They also began the long, ultimately unsuccessful job of trying to control the Vietnamese people.

3

The Nationalists

French control over Vietnam touched every aspect of Vietnamese life. Eager to reap a profit from its Asian possession, France systematically went about developing the country—from building roads to opening rubber plantations. At the same time, France broke down many Vietnamese traditions. The French believed that their own culture was the finest in the world—that they were doing the Vietnamese a favor by imposing the French systems of government, law, education, business. They also knew that the Vietnamese, their culture weakened, would have difficulty rebelling against French control.

Although an emperor was always on the throne, he had no power. Vietnamese citizens held few government positions, and those that they did hold were at the lower levels. Their salaries were also lower than those earned by Frenchmen who held equivalent or even lower positions.

Prior to the French takeover, much of the rural peasantry had been literate. The French wiped that out. By 1945, they had closed nearly twenty thousand schools established before 1858, and 80 percent of the Vietnamese were illiterate.[3] The Vietnamese who did receive schooling were required to write in

French or Quoc Ngu, the romanized writing system for the Vietnamese language developed by Alexandre de Rhodes in the mid-seventeenth century. Lessons were laden with French indoctrination.

In economic matters, Vietnam was made to produce what France wanted. Peasants who owned land lost it when the French took over their small plots to make large estates and rubber plantations. The peasants, now tenant farmers, gave up a large share of their yield as rent for the land. French interest in making money necessitated the building up of small industries and the roads, bridges, even a railroad, that were essential for moving goods. But the Vietnamese were the ones who paid for these improvements, in high taxes and forced labor.

Just as they had chafed under China's colonial rule, the Vietnamese chafed under France's domination. Not surprisingly, nationalists—Vietnamese citizens who longed for their country's independence—began to emerge.

Vietnam's most revered hero is a man who in later life went by the name Ho Chi Minh (pronounced Ho Chee Min), which means "He Who Enlightens." So mysterious are the qualities that make a great leader, so successful was Ho in motivating the Vietnamese, that even his enemies grudgingly respected him as one of the world's master politicians.

Ho was born Nguyen Sinh Cung (pronounced Win Sin Koong), in 1890, the son of a scholar and mandarin. His father, Nguyen Sinh Sac (Win Sin Sock), was fired by the French from his position in the imperial court because of his outspoken nationalism—he even refused to learn French. After leaving the emperor's court, Nguyen Sinh Sac traveled through the countryside, reciting Vietnamese lore to the peasants and giving medical treatment. Nonetheless, he encouraged his children to learn everything they could about France—its language and customs. Thus his son was armed for the struggle to come—the struggle to free Vietnam of all foreign domination.

A Vietnamese mandarin

Using the name Van Ba (pronounced Vahn Bah), Ho set sail in 1911 as a crewman on a freighter. His movements over the next several years are not known, although it is known that he spent some time in the United States. The biographical thread can be picked up again in 1915, when Ho began work as a pastry chef at London's Carlton Hotel under the famous Georges Auguste Escoffier. Two years later, he moved to Paris. There he was known as Nguyen Ai Quoc (Win Eye Kwahk), which means "Nguyen the Patriot." Working as a painter and photo-retoucher, he found in Paris many of his countrymen, who were being sent to France to help fight Germany in World War I.

Being in France was an eye-opener for the Vietnamese there. At home, they had seen only the rich French, who shared similar financial and political goals. Paris, on the other hand, was filled with poor as well as rich French citizens. Paris was also filled with people advocating all kinds of political ideas—even communism (see pages 91–93).

At the conclusion of the war, Ho went to Versailles, just outside Paris, where he hoped to meet U.S. President Woodrow Wilson. Ho was impressed by the Fourteen Points, principles Wilson proposed not just for the peace treaty with Germany but for a new world order. As such, the Fourteen Points addressed colonial issues, self-determination, and, of course, a League of Nations. Concerned about his homeland, Ho took with him a proposal for reforms in Indochina, but he could not get an interview with the president.

Stymied, Ho turned to Marxism and began writing in Paris for revolutionary papers and journals. Nikolai Lenin, then head of the Soviet Union, had decided to advance communism by fostering nationalist movements in colonies. Seeing Russia as a source of assistance for Vietnam's growing nationalism, Ho moved to Moscow in 1923. There he wrote for various publications while taking courses at the University of the Peoples of the East. He moved to China to act as interpreter for a Soviet adviser to General Chiang Kai-shek but was forced to flee in 1927 when Chiang turned against the Communists.

For more than ten years, Ho would move about eastern Europe and Asia, ceaselessly working to promote independence for Vietnam. Considered a troublemaker by the French as early as 1920, he was often only one step ahead of French police. Indeed, they had him in hand in Hong Kong in 1932, but he managed to escape. Kept in a prison infirmary because of tuberculosis, he arranged for a hospital worker to report him dead, then took off.

Not until 1940 did Ho return to Vietnam, where life had been very much altered by the start of World War II. France had been conquered by Germany earlier that year. Japan then demanded of France transit rights through Vietnam. In fact, Japan took control of Vietnam, using the French as administrators. What else could the French do? They did not want to give up their position in Indochina, but at the same time, their own government defeated, they were powerless to evict the Japanese. The Vietnamese now had two foreign oppressors. Sneaking into the country, Ho set up headquarters in a cave in northern Vietnam. From there, he and his followers called together other nationalists.

In May 1941, Ho and his followers established the Vietnam Doc Lap Dong Minh, which means the "League for Vietnamese Independence." Soon its members became known simply as the Vietminh. Ho shrewdly saw that they must rally all Vietnamese—peasants and mandarins alike. He carefully avoided references to communism; he did not want to alienate any Vietnamese nationalists, nor did he want to suggest that the organization would be directed by the Soviet Union—yet another foreign power.

During World War II, the Vietminh were being organized. Under Vo Nguyen Giap (pronounced Vo Win Zhahp), Ho's trusted associate, guerrillas were recruited and trained to harass the Japanese. So effective were the Vietminh that Americans working for the Office of Strategic Services (forerunner of the Central Intelligence Agency) gave Ho some assistance. Another important activity was to keep abreast of other nationalist groups in the country. Vietminh were carefully infiltrated into everything from religious sects to youth groups. The organization often helped other nationalist groups, but Ho Chi Minh was not above having his rivals assassinated or betrayed to the French police if their methods or goals were not compatible with his.

Over time the Vietminh became the strongest of the nationalist groups, by virtue of their very broad base. The Dai Viet, another group, looked for support mainly from the upper classes—people who wanted to protect their position while getting the foreigners out. The Vietminh, on the other hand, while not excluding the upper classes, drew their main support from the peasantry, who made up more than 80 percent of the population. Like the upper classes, they wanted the foreigners out. In addition, they wanted many social changes.

Fearful that the French might attempt to regain their control, the Japanese attacked and imprisoned French troops in Vietnam in March 1945. Then they reappointed Bao Dai (pronounced Bow, rhyming with *cow*, Dye), the last emperor under the French, as emperor of a free Vietnam—under Japanese control. When Japan lost World War II, in August of that same year, the Vietminh challenged Bao Dai. The emperor had little popular support among the Vietnamese, for he had permitted both the French and the Japanese to use him as a puppet—a sham ruler. Bao Dai abdicated, agreeing to serve as supreme adviser to Ho Chi Minh's government. On September 2, 1945, masses of Vietnamese cheered as Ho declared the independence of the Democratic Republic of Vietnam in a speech that made reference to the American Declaration of Independence.

A half-year later, Ho invited into his government another

nationalist, Ngo Dinh Diem. (His name is pronounced No Din Zee-em. Ngo is his family name; Diem, his given name. Following Vietnamese practice, he is referred to simply as Diem or, on formal occasions, as Ngo Dinh Diem. Ho is an exception to that rule.) Like Ho Chi Minh, Diem was born in central Vietnam, the son of a mandarin. Like Ho's father, Diem's father gave up his post at the imperial court; first mandarin to Emperor Thanh Thai (pronounced Tahn Tye), he refused to be a party to French manipulation. Diem, a Catholic, considered becoming a priest, but he decided instead on a government career. After graduating from the School of Law and Administration, in Hanoi, he became a provincial governor at age twenty-five. In that job, he distinguished himself as an honest, effective administrator. In 1933, Bao Dai, emperor since 1925, appointed Diem minister of the interior and head of a commission on administrative reform. The French, however, would not give the young administrator free rein to do his job. Diem quit, unwilling to be part of the charade, just as his father had. Watched closely by the French authorities, Diem retired to his family's home in Hue to spend some ten years in a private life of study. At the same time, he promoted an independent Vietnamese state through correspondence with people both inside and outside of his country. Threatened by Diem's nationalist efforts, the French sought him for arrest, which he eluded only with the assistance of the Japanese in 1944.

Ngo Dinh Diem turned down Ho Chi Minh's invitation to join his government. Just as he was a true nationalist, Diem was also a true anti-Communist. He had not liked what he had seen of communism, and he was personally touched by the horrors of the Communist effort, for the Vietminh had killed his brother Ngo Dinh Khoi (pronounced No Din Coy) earlier in 1945.

Five years later, when the Vietminh tried to kill him, Diem left Vietnam. Out of the country, he would not have to take a stand on who were more dreadful—the French or the Vietminh.

4

The Indochina War

At the end of World War II, Vietnam was not a happy place to be. With the Japanese defeated in the war, China and Great Britain were assigned the task of disarming and repatriating, or sending home, Japanese troops stationed in Vietnam. However, the Chinese troops responsible for the area north of the sixteenth parallel instead rampaged through the countryside. Adding to these miseries, a famine killed some two million people in the north. In Cochinchina, various Vietnamese groups were vying for power with the Vietminh. French colonials living there were vocal about saving their fortunes. Suddenly, French troops were available to protect their interests. Imprisoned by the Japanese since March 1945, the troops were released by Major General Douglas Gracey, commander of the British forces responsible for Vietnam south of the sixteenth parallel. The French were back on top.

Ho tried to negotiate with the French. As long as they would acknowledge Vietnam's independence, the French could carry on their businesses there. On May 31, 1946, Ho sailed for France to finalize an agreement. While he was on his way to

Europe, the French high commissioner for Indochina, Admiral Georges Thierry d'Argenlieu, declared Cochinchina a republic—an independent state ruled by its own people—separate from the rest of the country.

D'Argenlieu had acted on his own, but French government officials in Paris saw it in their best interest not to repudiate the declaration—Cochinchina accounted for the bulk of France's profits in Vietnam. They would get the weak Bao Dai to serve as chief of state, and the Frenchified upper-class Vietnamese who held government positions in Cochinchina, profiting as they did by their dealings with France, also could be depended upon. Ho, French officials realized, would not be so cooperative. They therefore agreed to recognize Vietnam as an independent state, but that Vietnam would not include the Republic of Cochinchina. So firmly did the Vietminh believe in sovereignty for all of Vietnam, so firmly did the French want to hold at least Cochinchina in their grip, that war was inevitable.

The first big flareup came on November 20, 1946, when the French asserted their right to collect customs duties. After a short truce, the French opened fire on the port city of Haiphong, forcing the Vietminh leaders—as well as Vietnamese civilians— to flee. Trouble then spread to Hanoi. Once again, the Vietminh leaders withdrew, this time to the countryside, where they would remain until 1954.

After taking over Hanoi in 1946, the French began to reach out into the Red River delta. They built forts as they took control of one area and then moved into new territory. Yet despite their fortifications and their superior armaments, the French troops were continually harassed. General Giap's guerrillas were as troublesome for the French as Le Loi's had been for the Chinese, more than five hundred years earlier.

Ho and Giap's Vietminh forces were not large at first. Nor were they well armed. But villagers, who recognized the Vietminh as the one group trying to evict the French, provided the guerrillas with safety and food. Although they lacked arms, the fighters had fervor. Giap used techniques developed by the Chinese Communists to build his own phenomenally solid, close-knit fighting units. The guerrillas were divided into groups of three, called cells. Within each cell, indoctrination was constant; always they were reminded that the enemy was France and its despised colonial rule. Along with indoctrination, self-criticism was a highly valued tool. Everyone, regardless of role or rank, was required to participate in reviews of his own and his fellow guerrillas' failings. This provided an effective way to improve tactics. Most important, self-criticism provided a way to bond the Vietminh, first to their cell, ultimately to the entire army. They were willing to die for one another and for the cause.

With their advantage in arms, the French still recognized the difficulty of their task. There was an immense area to cover, and the land, particularly with its dense jungles, was hard to get through. French troops, strung out far into rural areas, were often isolated. The Vietnamese population did not assist the French. In fact, General Jacques Philippe Leclerc believed the task to be impossible. "It would take 500,000 men to do it," he observed, "and even then it could not be done."[4] Nonetheless, he would try.

Skirmishing with the French, Giap's troops were able to pick up valuable equipment abandoned by them. But his arsenal was expanded dramatically in 1949 when China's Communist party, led by Mao Zedong, wrested control of China from Chiang Kai-shek. In addition to supplying arms, the Chinese Communists gave the Vietminh permission to train their guerrillas in China itself, safe from the French. Thus Giap put together an army.

The events in China gave a boost to France too. Prior to 1949, the United States had kept its distance from France's problems in Indochina—Americans had no interest in supporting colonialism. Mao Zedong's Communist victory in China

Vo Nguyen Giap (left) and Ho Chi Minh (right)

changed that. Having seen communism ruthlessly devour so many Eastern European countries, Americans feared the same thing would happen in Asia. So the United States began financing the French military effort. By 1954, the United States was paying 78 percent of France's Indochina war bill.[5]

Emerging from thin air to attack small units of French forces and then vanishing back into thin air, the Vietminh guerrillas kept the French busy. But General Giap wanted to wage conventional battles too. Victories in formal battles would help convince everyone—the Vietnamese, the French, the whole world—that the Vietminh were *the* force in Vietnam. Here Giap had his failures. Two major defeats came in 1951, one at Vinhyen, in January, and another at Haiphong, in March. A battle on the Day River in May proved a draw. The Vietminh were forced to withdraw, but the French were tired by the encounter as well.

For another two years, the French continued to fight off the Vietminh, but their hold on the country, particularly the rural areas, was weak. They had won many battles and killed many Vietminh fighters. Yet for those they killed, more were ready to take their place. In 1952, the French started to develop the Vietnamese troops fighting with them. But the French-Vietnamese army would never work well. Vietnamese soldiers were not adequately trained to handle the military defense of their country, and French soldiers were not prepared to trust the Vietnamese soldiers by their side.

As years went by with no victory in sight, French public opinion began to turn against the war in Indochina. Referring to it as *"la sale guerre"*—the dirty war—the French watched their army's casualty figures mount. Where would it end? they wondered. In Paris, the French government decided to seek a negotiated settlement. The Soviets had suggested that talks to be held in Geneva, Switzerland, to end the Korean war be expanded to cover Indochina. China, the Vietminh's arms supplier, pressed Ho to agree. Ho signaled his willingness to talk. The French government did too. But the French military leaders in Vietnam were still eager to lure Giap's forces into battle. Victory would reaffirm French superiority.

The place the French chose to stage their grand encounter was Dienbienphu. Close to the border of Laos, the village lay in a valley near Vietminh sanctuaries, or safe staging areas, and supply routes. Some French strategists pointed out that Dienbienphu was surrounded by mountains—a risk because military tactics always favor the higher ground. Other French strategists noted that Dienbienphu would be hard to resupply by airplanes in bad weather. Cocky, the French command dismissed the criticisms. The notion that Giap could besiege Dienbienphu was ridiculous. He did not have heavy artillery, and even if he did, how would he bring it into the area and set it up? Besides, the Vietminh were weak. Many of Giap's guerrillas were in other parts of the country. Even if the Vietminh could open a concentrated attack, they could not keep it up for long. The porters who carried in the supplies and equipment for the Vietminh army would have difficulty moving through the treacherous terrain. The rain and mud that come with the monsoons would make impossible the job of sustaining the army for a long battle. No, the French command said, a base at Dienbienphu could be held.

The French command was wrong. To encourage a battle he believed he could win, Giap had ordered light Vietminh attacks around the country, suggesting that his troops were far-flung. In the meantime, many other Vietminh fighters were preparing for Dienbienphu. Regiments spent weeks walking along jungle trails to get to their positions. Traveling during the night to avoid detection by French reconnaissance planes, thousands of porters pushed bicycles adapted to carry as much as five hundred pounds of supplies to the peaks surrounding Dienbienphu. Artillery was disassembled and carried over long distances, to be reassembled on the spot. The men dug bunkers in the hills. Well camouflaged, the bunkers were invisible to reconnaissance planes.

On March 13, 1954, the Vietminh began their attack by

sending rank upon rank of soldiers against the fort. Thousands of Vietminh fell in these human-wave attacks. Giap then opened up with heavy artillery. The first French artillery post was demolished early the next morning. Colonel Charles Piroth immediately recognized that all the artillery posts were incorrectly placed. In addition, they were not solid enough to withstand the Vietminh attack. Aghast at his miscalculated siting of the posts, the one-armed colonel withdrew to his quarters that evening, pulled the pin from a grenade with his teeth, and clutched the explosive to his breast. Suicide seemed the only honorable course left to him.

As some had predicted, French planes had difficulty resupplying the fort because of bad weather. Desperate, the French appealed to the United States for assistance. The opinion of American military leaders was split over what would be required to help the French, and President Eisenhower could not muster support for assistance in Congress. After the costly Korean War, American congressmen were unwilling to help the French unless there was support from other countries. None could be roused.

The Geneva Conference opened on April 26, 1954, first to discuss Korea. On May 7, the Vietminh captured Dienbienphu.

PART II

Americans Take to the Field of Battle

Eventually South Vietnam became, for all intents and purposes, a Communist-type country without communism. It had all the controls, all the oppressions and all the frustrating, grim aspects of the modern totalitarian state—without the dynamism, efficiency and motivation that communism had brought to the North.

—David Halberstam,
The Making of a Quagmire[1]

5

The Geneva Accords

The day after the Vietminh took Dienbienphu, May 8, 1954, nine delegations came together in Geneva, Switzerland, to consider the Indochina problem. As well as representatives from Laos and Cambodia, there were two groups from Vietnam—one representing the government of Bao Dai, the other representing the Vietminh. Another Asian delegation was that of Communist China. France, the colonial power in Indochina, was represented, and so were the United States, the Soviet Union, and England.

One would think that the Vietminh, having defeated the French at Dienbienphu, would have a lot to say about the terms of the peace agreement. But as it turned out, they did not fare well at all. Ironically, the Soviet Union and China put pressure on the Vietminh to accept much less than they might have expected. The Soviet Union, mindful of its own interests in Europe, favored France. China's reasons for pressuring the Vietminh were more long-range. Having just tangled with the United States in Korea, the Chinese were eager to keep the Americans from finding any other footholds in Asia. One way to do that was to ensure a French presence in Indochina. Further, the Chinese did not want Vietnam strong and unified—history had shown them how nettlesome that could be. So Zhou Enlai, head of the Chinese delegation, proposed partition—the separation of the country into two parts. The north would be controlled by the Vietminh; the south would be controlled by Bao Dai, whom the French had managed to appoint as chief of state in 1949. After two years, both zones would have elections to choose one political leadership for the entire country.

The country was temporarily divided at the seventeenth parallel, not far from the two walls across Quangtri that the Nguyen family had built more than three hundred years earlier. Troops were to regroup, the Vietminh drawing to the north of the line and the French to the south. In addition, the accords allowed for an exchange of war prisoners and a three-hundred-day period for civilians to move from the north to the south or vice versa, according to their wishes.

The Geneva accords put an end to the military conflict, but they did not solve the political conflict. Still, they established a date—July 1956—and a means—elections—by which the Vietnamese would be reunited. But history was to take a different course. The two zones were to harden into two states—North Vietnam, formally the Democratic Republic of Vietnam, and South Vietnam, formally the Republic of Vietnam. As prospects for their political settlement grew dimmer, the military conflict was to be reignited.

The Vietminh, having fought long and hard against the French, were disappointed to gain so little at the Geneva Conference. But they knew that the 1956 elections would give them control of the entire country. Similarly, Bao Dai was distressed by the results of the conference. He and his delegation believed that the French had sacrificed them. The Americans regarded the conference as a "disaster," for the Communists had gained the north if not the whole country, and they would have it all in

Pham Van Dong, head of the Vietminh delegation at the 1954 Geneva Conference

1956.[2] Neither Bao Dai's nor the United States's delegation signed the accords.

While the terms of the accords were being hammered out, Bao Dai appointed as his prime minister Ngo Dinh Diem, the man whom Ho Chi Minh had once wanted in his government. Diem was in many ways the perfect choice for the post Bao Dai gave him. He was intelligent. He had had experience working in the government. As a provincial governor, he had displayed ability and fairness. No one could doubt that he was a fervent nationalist. When Diem left Vietnam, in 1950, he spent much of the next four years in the United States. There he studied religion at the Maryknoll Institute; at the same time, he passionately made the case for Vietnamese independence with any people of power he could find—among them Cardinal Francis Spellman and Senators Mike Mansfield and John Kennedy. His fervent anticommunism was also well known.

The French, however, were not happy to see Diem in power. They saw him as unbending, and they feared he might make it difficult to salvage much of their economic and cultural interests.

The United States was also not sure about Diem. Americans who worked in Vietnam believed that Diem did not have the strength and popularity to lead the South. But he was the only one in a position to hold at least a part of the country in the Western camp, so the United States would support him.

Many Vietnamese saw Diem's Catholicism as the religion of the West and its colonial urges. They thought Diem had been out of the country at the wrong time. Away between 1950 and 1954, he had not had to take a side in the war for independence. Few South Vietnamese were on hand to greet their prime minister when he arrived in Saigon on July 7, 1954.

Both the French and the Vietminh began the military disengagement laid out by the Geneva accords. Some 50,000 Vietminh troops left the South and moved north of the seventeenth parallel. Vietminh political organizers, however, were permitted to remain in the South. The network developed for the battle with the French was still in place.

Many Vietminh fighters who had lived in what was now South Vietnam left behind their families, although about twenty thousand civilians moved north with them. But the number of civilians who moved from the North to the South was astounding. It is estimated that 860,000 people left their homes above the seventeenth parallel to move to the South. Catholics made up the vast majority—600,000—of those who moved.[3]

The government of North Vietnam did not hinder this migration. Actually, it was beneficial to the North. Food was scarce at that time, and now there were 860,000 fewer mouths to feed. The emigrants also left behind land, which could be redistributed among the people who stayed. Finally, the exodus meant the departure of many people who might have criticized the government.

Many Catholics left the North because they had helped the French. They had also been persecuted by their non-Catholic neighbors. The South, with a Catholic prime minister, would be a more hospitable place to live. But their flight from the North was to a great extent encouraged by the United States. In 1954, Edward Lansdale, a U.S. government specialist in counterinsurgency, the process by which rebellions are opposed, set up the Saigon Military Mission. This secret American organization had as its goal the creation of unrest in North Vietnam. Lansdale sent one part of his team into the North, an action completely against the rules of the Geneva accords. There they told Catholics that the Virgin Mary was moving to the South. Lansdale also hired soothsayers, who predicted bad years to come for Ho and the Vietminh, good years for Diem and his regime. But the soothsayers were wrong; there were bad years ahead for everyone.

6

The Two Vietnams

The next several years were years of organization in both Vietnams. Having proved they could wage a war, Ho and his government were now busy trying to run a government. Much of their country had been damaged by the war with the French, and rebuilding of roads and light industry would be extensive. The North would also have to deal with chronic food shortages, for much of Vietnam's food was grown in the South. The government had to import rice.

In 1955, a land-reform program was instituted, but it proved a disaster. Many people who owned even slightly larger-than-average pieces of land were depicted as evil. Some were killed by local Vietminh officials who had no sense of restraint.

The small plots awarded to individuals under the new program were insufficient to support a family. However, Bernard Fall, a French historian, suggests that Ho may have been willing to see food production fall for a while. Food shortages would be an emphatic proof that privately owned small plots were not feasible. When the peasants recognized this—and hunger is a painful state that makes itself felt immediately—they would more readily embrace collectivization—that is, the creation of large state-owned areas of land to be worked by large groups of people.[4]

So disruptive was the situation that in 1956 North Vietnam experienced uprisings. These were quickly quelled. Ho stepped in to calm the situation. The land-reform regulations were loosened, and Ho acknowledged that the government had been wrong. Still, farmers who had suffered at the hands of local officials were bitter.

In the South, Ngo Dinh Diem was also attempting to get his country under control. One of his first efforts was to put the Binh Xuyen out of business. The Binh Xuyen was a group of government officials, businessmen, and crime bosses who controlled the bordellos and opium dens of Saigon. A sort of Vietnamese mafia, the group had its own armed squads who were happy to work as hired guns for anyone who needed such services. The showdown came in April 1955, when Diem ordered the army to attack the group's strongholds. After several days of fighting, which turned Saigon's streets into a battlefield and killed hundreds of innocent citizens, the Binh Xuyen was crushed. Diem had prevailed—at least for the time being. Impressed, the United States decided to support Diem wholeheartedly.

Diem, however, was not above the lawlessness of the Binh Xuyen. In October 1955, he held a referendum by which Bao Dai was deposed. Declaring himself president of the Republic of Vietnam, Diem claimed 98.2 percent of the vote, but the election was hardly fair. People who were expected to vote for Bao Dai were harassed, even beaten up, by government agents. In some voting areas, including Saigon, the number of votes cast was larger than the number of people eligible to vote.

Ngo Dinh Diem's brother Ngo Dinh Nhu (pronounced No Din New) was the mastermind behind the rigged election. Edward Lansdale, as head of the secret Saigon Military Mission, gave valuable assistance. For example, he helped design the ballots to the regime's advantage. Ballots for Diem were red, the color signifying good luck; those for Bao Dai were green, the color representing bad luck. By these means, Diem became a president in title but a dictator in fact.

The year 1955 was also marked by the first of Diem's aggressive efforts to rid the South of any remaining Vietminh. His agents scoured the countryside to find them. In the process, they introduced terrorism by the government. Diem's officials roamed throughout South Vietnam killing people on arrest or sending them off to prison camps, where they remained without a trial. Many of the regime's representatives used their powers to settle personal scores. With corruption and methods such as these, Diem would not easily gain his people's love or loyalty.

Even American diplomats often found the Diem regime difficult to support. The regime was an oligarchy—a system of rule by a very small, close-knit group. Assisting Ngo Dinh Diem in Saigon was Ngo Dinh Nhu, who served as Diem's chief political adviser and managed agents installed in every government department to watch for possible traitors and budding plots against the regime. Nhu's outspoken, volatile wife acted as her bachelor brother-in-law's first lady, but her influence extended far beyond the social sphere. It was Madame Nhu who pressed Diem to enact morality laws that flew in the face of traditional, firmly held Vietnamese values. Those new laws that did not tear the fabric of Vietnamese custom were simply irksome. One banned the sentimental popular songs the Vietnamese loved. The music, according to Madame Nhu, was not sufficiently anti-Communist. Another brother, Ngo Dinh Thuc (pronounced No Din Tuck), was archbishop of Hue, on the central Vietnam coast. Thuc nonetheless spent considerable time in Saigon, not only working on the management of church properties, but also helping his brothers run the government.

In tightening his control, Diem did much to weaken the country. The Ngos looked to the Catholics who had emigrated

Ngo Dinh Diem at the polls

from the North for much of their support, and, to keep that support, they gave them jobs and other favors. Fearful of being overthrown, the Ngos gave high military and government positions to people who had demonstrated loyalty to the regime. Ability was of secondary importance.

In the summer of 1956, the regime abolished elections for village chiefs and municipal councils. Diem gave as his excuse the problem of security. He pointed out that there were many Communist sympathizers living in the South, who could gain control by running for office. The decision allowed Diem to appoint whomever he liked to run the villages. The peasants were not happy. Diem had done away with a long established tradition of local government. The Vietnamese adage "The emperor's rule stops at the village gate," which accurately described a centuries-old way of life, no longer held true. Further, the peasants did not like the people Diem appointed. Often from other parts of the country, these officials knew nothing about the people they were appointed to govern.

The Americans, eager to see the southern regime grow in strength, believed strongly in the importance of land reform, as a way both to strengthen the economy and to win the allegiance of the peasants. The vast majority of Vietnamese were peasants, and Vietnam's economic power lay in its lush, fertile soil. High taxes and land ownership limited to the very rich had reduced the peasants to paupers. Prodded by the United States, Diem finally instituted a land-reform program in 1956. It was a failure. The plan was so poorly laid out that little land was distributed. At the same time, the program made both peasants and landowners angry with the regime.

For the Ngos, control of the government was still not enough. They tolerated no criticism of their policies, and to silence criticism, they prevented many newspapers from publishing. Even private citizens seemed threatening. When eighteen prominent South Vietnamese wrote to Diem politely urging reform before it was too late, they were arrested.

In 1956, the elections in both the North and the South called for by the Geneva accords did not take place. Ngo Dinh Diem refused to hold them. He justified his stand on three grounds: first, he maintained that tight Communist control of the North made an honest vote there impossible; second, he maintained that Communist guerrillas in the South made fair elections there equally impossible; and, finally, he maintained that South Vietnam was not bound by the terms of the Geneva accords because Bao Dai had not signed them.

Diem was supported in his decision by the United States. Even President Eisenhower acknowledged that Ho Chi Minh was so popular in both the North and South that the Communists would win in a free election.[5]

7

The Insurgency Begins

The North Vietnamese felt betrayed when it became clear that there would not be elections as mandated by the Geneva accords. They had agreed to partition reluctantly, and only because it was to have been temporary. Permanent division of their country was unacceptable for practical as well as ideological reasons. Vietnam worked well as one country, for the northern section, with its skilled labor, light industry, and a wealth of raw materials, complemented the southern area, which was oriented mostly to agriculture.

At the time, North Vietnam had more than enough problems of its own. The country could not wage a war against the South. In 1957 and 1958, the North Vietnamese proposed to Diem that relations between the North and South be normalized. Not only did they hope to buy food produced in the South; they also wished to enable Vietminh fighters who had moved to the North and their families who had remained in the South to visit one another. Diem did not even respond to the offers. If he had, there might still be two Vietnams. The Diem regime forced the North to try for reunification.

Diem's decision not to hold elections also caused bitterness among nationalists in the South. His campaign to root out the Vietminh had been extremely successful—by 1957, 90 percent of the Vietminh cells remaining in the Mekong delta had been destroyed.[6] Still, a few survived, and veterans of the war against the French found many discontented Southerners who were eager to join their cause.

Their goal was to bring about the collapse of the government of South Vietnam, the only serious impediment to re-unification. With this in mind, the insurgents began in 1957 gradually to move into the villages, taking positions in the local government or setting up what is called a parallel hierarchy—a full government staff ready to take over when the established government falls. Those local officials, teachers, and citizens who stoutly resisted their presence were assassinated.

At the same time, the insurgents set out to woo the peasants. They helped them in the rice paddies and established schools for their children. They also gave the peasants land belonging to absentee landowners—an unofficial land-reform program that cost the insurgents not a penny.

In 1960, the old Vietminh political organizers who had remained in the South and their new Southern recruits formed the National Liberation Front, or NLF. It was intended to draw together everyone in the South who wanted to see the country reunified. The Diem regime called them the Vietcong, which means "Viet Communists." Members of the NLF were angered by the nickname. They maintained that the NLF was not a Communist organization but a nationalist organization. The writer Frances FitzGerald has observed that few of the guerrillas knew much about Communist theory.[7] On the other hand, it is recognized that the NLF was firmly directed by the government of North Vietnam, which was clearly Communist.

The guerrillas used the age-old Vietnamese tradition of melting into the rural population for protection—Mao Zedong compared it to fish finding safety just by swimming in the sea. Who was to say that the guerrilla was not simply another innocent peasant? Control of a village did not mean that the Vietcong were always there and always in charge. Control of a village meant that the Vietcong could move back in whenever they wanted—because the villagers either liked having them there or were so frightened by them as to cooperate. By 1962, the Vietcong would be established in 80 percent of all of South Vietnam.[8]

When John Kennedy was elected president of the United States in November 1960, he shared many Americans' views about the world order: the very real, albeit nonmilitary, hostility of Cold War was a result of the spread of communism, which threatened to consume all of the world; the United States, as the world's most powerful nation, must assist all freedom-loving peoples in their efforts to resist communism.

When Kennedy took office in January 1961, he found that plans had been begun during the previous administration, that of President Dwight D. Eisenhower, for an invasion of Cuba, a Communist country under the control of Fidel Castro. The attempt was made in April 1961. The Bay of Pigs invasion, as it was called because of the focus of the attack, was a terrible failure, and both Kennedy and the United States looked foolish and weak. It was not an auspicious beginning for Kennedy's administration. Further, the spread of communism had not been curbed.

Kennedy's first public confrontation with a Communist leader took place several months later. In June 1961, he met Nikita Khrushchev, prime minister of the Soviet Union, at a summit conference in Vienna, Austria. There the new president was put off balance by the ranting old Communist pro. After this encounter, Kennedy felt even more strongly that he must show the world that the United States would stand firm. Coming away from the conference, he observed to James Reston, a reporter

Vietcong guerrillas on the move.

for *The New York Times*: "Now we have a problem in making our power credible, and Vietnam is the place."[9]

The one problem with Vietnam as the place to display American power was Diem. Although no one could doubt Diem's passionate hatred of communism, no one could really point to his love of democracy. In the seven years that he had been running South Vietnam, he had held one clearly rigged election, he had stifled public discussion of policy, and he had abused many Southerners under the guise of cleaning out Communist guerrillas. The peasant's lot had not been bettered. Wealthy Vietnamese and Catholics continued to profit from the favoritism shown them by the regime. Corruption flourished. Filled with a sense of his rightness, Diem saw his role in the historical Vietnamese tradition. As head of state, he, Diem, held the Mandate of Heaven, just as the old emperors had. The people were to trust him. He had no obligation to consult them about his decisions.

American diplomats were able to see Diem and present their views and ideas. After all, the U.S. government had been pouring vast amounts of money into South Vietnam since 1955, paying for the training of the army and the like, so Diem had to give these diplomats a hearing. But he rarely accepted their recommendations, and he was able to mute the diplomats by suggesting that their proposed reforms concerned South Vietnam's internal affairs, which were none of their business. Fearful of being seen as a new breed of colonialists, the Americans could not press their views.

By 1961, the National Liberation Front was gaining control of the rural areas of South Vietnam. American officials in Vietnam believed that, to win the people's support, the government must offer them protection. They urged Diem to commit the army, which was known as the ARVN (the acronym for the Army of the Republic of Vietnam, pronounced Ar-vin), to making the villages safe. The peasants, having insignificant security forces within their village organization, could not keep the Vietcong out. Once in the villages, Americans asserted, the Vietcong could get from the peasants the money and rice that the guerrillas needed for their own survival.

So the ARVN set out to protect the villages, but they did so in a way sure to anger the peasants, for the soldiers were not above stealing chickens and rice for themselves, and they were likely to flee when skirmishes with the Vietcong occurred. Over the years, various efforts were made to help the peasants secure their villages: Agrovilles, the Staley plan, the Strategic Hamlet program, New Life Hamlets, the Hearts and Minds program—all are different names for essentially the same process. Villages were to be fortified and the peasants trained to protect them. But in many instances, peasants were forcibly moved from their villages. Their homes were then burned, and the ground was plowed to destroy the dark maze of underground tunnels the Vietcong dug for hiding places and escape routes. For the Vietnamese, a nation of ancestor worshipers, this was an especially cruel tactic. Generations before them had inhabited the same village—their bodies were buried in the same rice fields. For a peasant to be moved was to be severed from the past—from the source of one's identity.

With the dramatic rise in guerrilla incidents in 1961, Kennedy decided that an increase in the number of American military advisers would help the ARVN. He also looked to the technology of war to improve the situation. In February 1962, two U.S. Army air support units were sent to South Vietnam. This raised the number of American advisers in Vietnam from 685, the limit on foreign advisers permitted by the Geneva accords, to 4,000. It also introduced the helicopter to the Vietnamese struggle.

Helicopters had many advantages. Once a group of guerrillas was located, a flock of helicopters would take off from an ARVN base. Helicopters in the lead would hover above the area, firing artillery so that helicopters in the rear, carrying troops, could land safely. After the skirmish, helicopters would ferry

49

the troops back to their bases. It was a novel form of warfare—commuter warfare.

With the added personnel and equipment came General Paul D. Harkins as head of the Military Assistance Command, Vietnam (MACV, pronounced Mac-vee). General Harkins firmly believed that the South Vietnamese could learn to put down the Communist guerrillas by themselves, and he also believed that Americans should be optimistic about the effort. When news correspondents talked with Americans in the field, however, they heard quite a different story—that the Vietcong were good fighters, that the ARVN leaders were poor fighters, and that the Vietcong were making progress.

The infusion of advisers and the introduction of helicopters made 1962 a good year for the ARVN. But the South Vietnamese, eager to please their American sponsors, also submitted inflated numbers for enemy dead, weapons captured, and the like. These figures Harkins accepted without question. When correspondents challenged the numbers quoted and the success of the military effort, Harkins reacted with great displeasure.

A battle that proved particularly discomfiting for the ARVN and its U.S. advisers occurred on January 2, 1963, at Ap-bac, a village in the Mekong delta close to Saigon. Vietcong companies had been spotted in the area several days before, and plans were made to engage them. But the date was set for the second so that American pilots could enjoy a festive New Year's Eve. That delay enabled the Vietcong, who had learned of the operation, to prepare their defenses. The Vietcong were a tenacious enemy who had learned how to disable helicopters. They also continued to demonstrate an almost fanatical willingness to die for their cause, which the ARVN soldiers could not match.

Outnumbered ten to one, the Vietcong at Apbac nonetheless prevailed. They held their fire until most of the ARVN troops had been dropped off by the helicopters. Then they let loose. Five helicopters were disabled. Many ARVN soldiers then lost their lives because of a slow, poorly planned attempt to rescue the helicopter crews. The South Vietnamese commander of the ARVN infantrymen moving in from the south refused to continue when one of his officers was killed. More ARVN soldiers died when paratroopers entered the fray at twilight; in the gathering dusk, the South Vietnamese found they were battling one another. Meanwhile, the Vietcong had slipped away.

The battle at Apbac, though only one of thousands of encounters with the Vietcong, came to symbolize what was difficult about the Vietnam War. First, the leaders of the ARVN were often unwilling to do battle, and Americans, serving as advisers, could not order them to do anything. Second, though the American advisers in the field recognized the battle as a clear victory for the Vietcong, the higher-ups at MACV, in Saigon, chose to see it as a victory for the ARVN. They interpreted the outcome by conventional military standards, seeing the Vietcong as the losers because they had left the scene. But the Vietcong were not fighting a conventional war, in which success is measured by territory won and held. They were fighting a political war based on insurgency, in which success is measured by a growing awareness among the citizens that their current government, in this case the American-supported Diem regime, has neither the desire nor the ability to fulfill its responsibilities.

8

The Coup

While the Diem regime was fighting the Vietcong in guerrilla battles in the countryside, it felt increasingly powerful opposition in the cities—opposition that was fragmented until the spring of 1963.

Since his return to Vietnam in the summer of 1954, Diem's position had been regularly challenged. The challenges came from his own military leaders. As early as the fall of 1954, ARVN commanders were laying plans for a coup d'état—an overthrow of the regime by force. Edward Lansdale cleverly foiled that plot. Thereafter, Diem took great care to appoint ARVN commanders who were completely loyal to him. Still, other plots followed. In November 1960, another coup by the military failed. In February 1962, two pilots in the South Vietnamese air force bombed the presidential palace in Saigon. Diem and his family miraculously emerged safe and sound—and still in power.

Finally, Buddhist monks provided the glue for opposition to the Diem regime. On May 8, 1963, the Buddhists in Hue gathered to celebrate the birth of Buddha. There the government enforced an old law that prohibited the flying of Buddhist flags. This sparked long-simmering resentments. The Buddhists had endured centuries of persecution, first by the emperors, who saw them as a threat to their Confucianist state; then by the French, who had come in part to spread Christianity; and then by Diem, who favored his fellow Catholics. When the Buddhists peacefully gathered at the radio station in Hue to hear a speech by Thich (pronounced Tick, it means "venerable") Tri Quang (pronounced Tree Kwahng), a Buddhist bonze, or monk, they were fired upon by police and ARVN troops. Nine people died, either shot or trampled. The incident set off demonstrations throughout the South.

The climax of this unrest came on June 11, when Thich Quang Duc (pronounced Tick Kwahng Duck), an older Buddhist monk, sat down in a busy intersection in Saigon, was doused with gasoline by another Buddhist, and was set afire by yet another. Malcolm Browne, a photographer for the Associated Press, had been told the day before that something would happen, so when Thich Quang Duc burned himself to death, Browne was on the scene with his camera. The ritual proved disturbing to people all around the world. Seeing photographs of the event on their television screens and in their newspapers, images that would endure in their minds to this day, they wondered about what was happening in South Vietnam.

The astonishing image of a man in saffron-colored robes consumed in flames was reinforced by a sophisticated public-relations campaign carried on by the militant Buddhists at the Xa Loi pagoda, in Saigon. Turning out leaflets and political tracts, the religious center was the scene of press conferences that were sometimes held twice a day.

The self-immolation frightened Diem, who saw this stunning act as a threat to his power. Diem seized on the Buddhists' careful handling of the press as a way to dismiss the bonze's death as a public-relations ploy. He even suggested that Thich Quang Duc had been bribed by NBC television so that the network could offer its American audience dramatic film footage in its news broadcasts. Madame Nhu shrilly dismissed the event as a "barbecue."[10]

Through the summer of 1963, the Buddhists were able to keep up the pressure, with more immolations by Buddhist bonzes and nuns and demonstrations that included people other than Buddhists. American diplomats counseled Diem to try to improve the regime's relationship with the Buddhists, but as in so many other instances, Diem told the Americans not to meddle in internal Vietnamese affairs.

On August 21, Ngo Dinh Nhu, Diem's brother, ordered the Vietnamese Special Forces, disguised as ARVN troops, to storm pagodas throughout the South. Buddhist monks and nuns were arrested, injured, or killed. Later, thousands of students protesting the raids were also arrested. Nhu had hoped that the raids would solve two of his problems at once: the militant Buddhists and their followers who were fanning the flames of unrest would be rounded up; at the same time, the public would blame the ARVN for the attack—without public support, the ARVN would not dare attempt a coup against the regime.

But no one was fooled about who had carried out the raids on the pagodas. The Kennedy administration decided the United States would no longer support Diem if Nhu was part of his brother's government. The Buddhist crisis had succeeded in uniting Buddhists and non-Buddhists against the Diem regime.

Just after the August pagoda raids, Henry Cabot Lodge replaced Frederick Nolting as the United States ambassador to South Vietnam. In describing the situation in Saigon to government officials in Washington, Lodge confirmed that ARVN officers were again busily at work on another coup. But the generals would not attempt a coup if it threatened loss of American support—both the money and the advisers. The United States believed that Diem was not doing a good job of leading his country, but were the generals equal to the task? The United

A procession of Buddhist bonzes several weeks after Thich Quang Duc's self-immolation

States was not eager to see Diem ousted if the generals could not set up a government. Without a government, South Vietnam would be unable to continue the war against communism.

At about the same time, Kennedy sent two representatives, Major General Victor Krulak and Joseph A. Mendenhall, on a fact-finding tour of South Vietnam. Krulak, a military man, based his observations on reports from the military. He spoke with American and ARVN officers, who believed that, in time, the Vietcong could be defeated. The ARVN was big, and American training and equipment would turn the tide, Krulak reported upon his return. Mendenhall returned home with much less hope. A State Department employee who had once worked in Vietnam, he spoke not with military leaders but with government officials in the cities. From them, he gathered a sense of despair that the political situation under Diem was so bad that the country was near collapse.

Krulak and Mendenhall's report to the president was an example of the widely varying views people held about Vietnam. In fact, Kennedy was prompted to ask the two, "You guys did visit the same country, didn't you?"[11]

Early in October, the ARVN generals talked again with American officials in Saigon. The generals said that they were firmly committed to a coup, and while they did not want American assistance, they did want assurances that the United States would not thwart the coup. Further, they wanted a pledge that American financial assistance—then more than half a billion dollars a year—would not end.

The generals' approach was perfect for American purposes. They did not ask for permission to stage a coup, nor did they ask for Americans to take part in pulling it off. The U.S. could—and did—disavow all responsibility for the coup later.

The coup began on the afternoon of November 1, 1963, when ARVN units surrounded the presidential palace. Diem and Nhu moved to an air-conditioned shelter in the cellar, calm in the belief that they would be protected by soldiers loyal to them. The generals telephoned Diem to say that he and Nhu could leave the country. If they refused, the military would attack the palace. Diem telephoned ARVN commanders he thought were loyal to him, but none came to his assistance.

That same evening at about eight, as the presidential palace guards battled to protect them, Diem and Nhu slipped away through a tunnel and fled to Cholon, the Chinese suburb of Saigon. The next morning, Diem realized that the coup had succeeded, and he accepted the generals' suggestion that he and Nhu leave the country.

The generals sent an armored car to transport the Ngo brothers from St. Xavier Church to the ARVN staff headquarters. While being driven back to Saigon, Ngo Dinh Diem and his brother were shot and stabbed repeatedly. The people of South Vietnam celebrated the end of a hated regime.

But there was turmoil all over the world. Three weeks later, John Kennedy also was assassinated. In December 1963, the Hanoi regime began to consider if the time had come to concentrate on its bid for control over all of Vietnam.

PART III

The American War in Vietnam

We saw [the Vietcong] now dying by the thousands all over the country, yet they didn't seem depleted, let alone exhausted. . . .

—*Michael Herr,*
Dispatches[1]

9

President Johnson's War

President Kennedy was a man of immense intelligence and charm, and when he died, Americans grieved.

Vice-President Lyndon Johnson worked quickly to pick up the reins of government—a difficult task. Part of the difficulty lay in the unexpectedness of Kennedy's death; Johnson had no time to prepare for some aspects of his job as president. Ironically, another part of the difficulty lay in the nature of the vice-presidency; historically, vice-presidents have not played a central role in U.S. administrations, and Johnson was no exception to that rule.

Nonetheless, he immediately set out to reassure people at home and abroad that the government would continue to function smoothly. To that end, five days after taking office he restated American resolve: "This nation will keep its commitments from South Vietnam to West Berlin."[2]

One of the tantalizing what-ifs in history is what Kennedy would have done about Vietnam if he had lived. He had recognized that the government of South Vietnam was not strong. He had also recognized that while the United States could help in

61

this fight against communism, the war was ultimately South Vietnam's war, to be won or lost by the South Vietnamese. Early in 1963, Charles de Gaulle, president of France, had warned Kennedy that the Vietnam conflict would prove "a bottomless military and political swamp" for the United States.[3] As both a Frenchman and a soldier, de Gaulle was someone whose advice was well worth weighing. Perhaps Kennedy agreed with de Gaulle; some months before his death, he confided to Mike Mansfield, the Senate majority leader, that Vietnam was a losing proposition and that he would get the U.S. out—but not before the 1964 elections.[4]

When Lyndon Johnson took office, the troublesome Diem government had been replaced by a junta, or interim government, composed of four generals. Ambassador Lodge had cabled Washington shortly after the coup saying, "The prospects now are for a shorter war."[5] To Johnson, a proud president of a proud world power, that sounded fine. He was eager to halt the spread of communism. That, after all, had been United States policy since the end of World War II. Even so, he was not about to jump in with both feet. A gifted politician, Johnson had developed great skill in shaping domestic programs. But he was aware of how little experience he had in foreign affairs. He decided to postpone decisions about Vietnam for as long as he could. That would give him time to consider all the possibilities.

Johnson also worried about how the situation in Vietnam might affect the work he was truly interested in: the social legislation that formed what is called the Great Society program for Americans. A war would distract congressmen from the legislation he wished to present. A war would also tie up money needed to fund the Great Society programs.

Johnson began by trying to figure out how to wage a war quietly. In the spring of 1964, his staff drafted a resolution by which Congress would give to the president its support and approval for any reaction to Vietcong aggression he felt was

Lyndon Johnson (right) standing next to Nguyen Van Thieu, who was elected president of the Republic of Vietnam in 1967

needed. At that time, Johnson decided against sending the draft to Congress for fear that it would provoke too much debate. There being no crisis just then, congressmen might balk at giving the president such powers.

Johnson finally found his opening to Congress in August 1964. The events that sparked passage of the resolution took place in the Gulf of Tonkin, off of North Vietnam. There, the *Maddox*, an American destroyer, was simulating attacks on North Vietnam. When the North Vietnamese turned on their radar, the *Maddox* could locate their radar installations. Three North Vietnamese patrol boats went after the *Maddox*, but they did not damage the ship.

The next day, August 3, the *Maddox* and another destroyer, the *C. Turner Joy*, were ordered back to the same area. The North Vietnamese appeared again. The weather was foul, and there was some question whether the destroyers were fired upon. John Herrick, captain of the *Maddox*, was not at all sure. He reported as follows:

> Review of action makes many recorded contacts and torpedoes fired appear doubtful. Freak weather effects and overeager sonarman may have accounted for many reports. . . .[6]

President Johnson did not wait to find out just what—if anything—had happened. He called in members of Congress and told them the *Maddox* had been attacked again. He did not mention the *Maddox*'s simulated attacks on North Vietnam. He informed the congressmen that he would punish the North Vietnamese for this incident by bombing four patrol-boat bases and an oil depot. Then he pulled out the resolution drafted by his aides some months earlier and asked Congress to pass it.

Throughout American history, Congress has generally laid aside party politics to support the president when there has been a threat from another country. In this instance, the same thing happened. Johnson's resolution was quickly passed by Congress. Senators and representatives who were disturbed by the broadness of the resolution were persuaded not to propose amendments—no one wanted to tie the president's hands. Congressmen to whom it was not at all clear what the trouble in Vietnam was about went along too; not to vote for the resolution seemed unpatriotic. So, what came to be known as the Gulf of Tonkin Resolution was passed resoundingly. Only two dissenting votes were cast in the Senate. The resolution was approved unanimously in the House of Representatives.

Johnson was elated. In effect, he had received permission from Congress to do whatever he chose in Vietnam. Eight months later, he looked back on the confusion about the *Maddox*'s second day in the Gulf of Tonkin and confided to a friend, "For all I know, our navy was shooting at whales."[7]

Johnson did not make immediate use of his new war powers, for 1964 was an election year. His opponent was Barry Goldwater, a firm advocate of military muscle—during the campaign, Goldwater proposed all-out bombing of North Vietnam. Many Americans believed that Goldwater was a dangerous man who would use weaponry too quickly, too harshly. Johnson did not want to escalate the war at that time. A strong but restrained stance on Vietnam would keep him free of the militaristic taint Goldwater could not shake. The policy paid off. Lyndon Johnson was elected to the presidency with an astonishing 61 percent of the vote. His was the greatest electoral landslide in the history of the American presidency.

With the election behind him, Johnson had to begin making decisions about Vietnam. The Vietcong continued to be effective despite the American military advisers and sophisticated U.S. weapons in South Vietnam. Further, North Vietnam had begun sending soldiers from its regular army to help the guerrillas in the South in mid-1964. Finally, the political situation in South

Vietnam had grown messier. The military junta that took over after the coup against Diem lasted less than three months. It was itself overthrown late in January 1964. Six other changes of government followed in the course of a year.

What were the possibilities? The United States could simply pull out, but then we would look weak. Such an action, it was believed, would encourage the spread of communism, not only in Vietnam but elsewhere in the world. Another possibility was to send American combat troops to Vietnam. But the military, with recollections of the Korean War, was not eager for another land war in Asia. Nor were Johnson and his aides eager for the hue and cry that Americans would raise. Yet another possibility was to bomb North Vietnam.

Those who favored bombing saw any number of advantages. They believed that it would force the Hanoi leadership to reconsider its decision to send North Vietnamese soldiers to fight in the South. They also pointed out that it would slow the movement of matériel—the war supplies and equipment with which the North kept the Vietcong in business. In the process, bombing would destroy the factories, supply depots, and transportation network that the North had worked so hard to rebuild after the war with the French. Bombing would break the will of the North Vietnamese and at the same time encourage the South Vietnamese to carry on the struggle. If the North was bombed, they said, North Vietnam—and the world—would see that the United States was serious about its commitment to South Vietnam.

But many in the Johnson administration doubted that bombing North Vietnam would work. The war, these aides asserted, was being fought—and lost—in the South, and that was where the United States should concentrate its energies. They pointed out that North Vietnam was basically a rural, farming country. Military installations were small and dispersed, making them both hard to bomb and not very significant when taken individually. A study of the bombing of Germany during World War II had shown it to be considerably less effective than had been supposed. Bombing had not put an end to the German ability to make and move matériel. Nor had it lowered the German will to fight—in fact, the Germans had pulled together with vastly increased morale. North Vietnam was intent on reunifying Vietnam, these aides warned. They would give up their industry and their lives for the cause.

There were other disadvantages. Those who cautioned against bombing went on to say that, if unsuccessful, bombing is difficult to end, for that admits failure. Bombing a country that had no air force and therefore no way to respond might also outrage people all around the world—not just the North Vietnamese. In both cases, the United States would be humiliated. Finally, would bombing bring what was referred to as flashpoint—that level of escalation that would finally draw China or Russia into the fight, perhaps setting off World War III?

10

Escalation

In the end, bombing was chosen. Called Operation Rolling Thunder, it began on March 21, 1965, and continued with few breaks for more than three years.

Assessed eight weeks after it was started, the bombing proved a failure. The North Vietnamese continued to pour men and matériel into South Vietnam. To American military leaders, this seemed incredible. They urged that the list of targets be expanded. So, with confidence in what technology could do, the Americans chose to bomb more and bomb harder.

At the same time the bombing of the North was begun, the first American combat troops went to South Vietnam. Two marine battalions—3,500 soldiers—were sent to Danang, arriving on March 8, 1965. Their mission was to protect the planes used for bombing, but their arrival opened the door to the possibility of Americans' taking on the battle against the Vietcong.

General Maxwell Taylor, who took over as U.S. ambassador to South Vietnam in June 1964, was against this use of American troops. He believed the American forces would not be well received by Vietnamese peasants. How could American soldiers

U.S. paratroopers taking up their positions

distinguish South Vietnamese civilians from Vietcong guerrillas? Further, he believed the ARVN would simply turn the war over to the Americans. The burden of fighting, Taylor repeated, should be entirely on the South Vietnamese. Although we could help them with advice and equipment, we couldn't wage and win the war for them.

But the pressure on Johnson to use American troops in combat was very strong. He believed the United States *must* succeed in Vietnam. He did not want communism to spread, and he did not want the United States to be viewed as weak. The South Vietnamese were not doing well, but a mighty nation like the United States would make short work of the poorly armed Vietcong guerrillas and their sponsor, small, underdeveloped North Vietnam. U.S. military officials kept saying the war was winnable. All that was needed was a bit more help.

So the mission of the U.S. troops in South Vietnam was changed in June 1965, and more troops were sent. General William Westmoreland, the commander of the U.S. forces in South Vietnam, believed that the ARVN, very much weakened by its skirmishes with the Vietcong, was spread too thin. They could not fight the Vietcong and at the same time secure the villages. Westmoreland put together what was called the search-and-destroy strategy. American troops would seek out and go to battle against the insurgents—both the Vietcong guerrillas and the North Vietnamese regular army units. The South Vietnamese troops would pacify the villages, ridding them of Vietcong and helping the peasants to develop their own militias and fortifications to protect themselves.

In effect, the Americans were taking over the war, and the number of American troops in South Vietnam quickly rose over the course of 1965 to close to 200,000. Up and up the numbers went. In late 1966, nearly 400,000 troops were in South Vietnam. By the end of 1967, nearly 500,000 troops were there.

American bombing in North Vietnam did provoke considerable criticism around the world. But the American bombing and defoliation—that is, the killing of vegetation to expose Vietcong hiding places—in South Vietnam was far more devastating. Along with the insurgents' hiding places and cover, it destroyed the homes, food source, the very lives, of many South Vietnamese peasants. A flood of refugees soon washed through the country.

Johnson was well aware that the military effort would be worthless if the South Vietnamese government could not make the country a place its own people would defend. In February 1966, Johnson flew to Honolulu to meet with Nguyen Cao Ky (pronounced Win Cow Key), South Vietnam's prime minister. Ky agreed to a variety of programs—from land reform to refugee assistance—that Johnson considered essential for winning the war. But ultimately, the insurgents had to be stopped. "I want to see those coonskins hanging on the wall," Johnson told Ky.[8]

All the while, American military leaders in South Vietnam maintained that the war was winnable—though it would take time. They pushed for more and more troops, urging Johnson to call up the reserves. Calling up the reserves would require a declaration of war, and the war was becoming extremely unpopular with the American people. Colleges and universities across the United States had become the scene of demonstrations that sometimes grew ugly, and many adults were beginning to join students in protesting American involvement in Vietnam.

Even some members of the Johnson administration had begun to wonder if the war was winnable. Robert McNamara, secretary of defense since 1961, had displayed, early in the war, considerable optimism that the United States could win. Previously president of Ford Motor Company, McNamara brought to his job a faith in what could be accomplished with technology and careful management. But over the years he saw that all of the money and all the men the United States had poured into

South Vietnam had not done anything to diminish the strength of the insurgents. Late in 1967, Johnson realized that McNamara had become a dove. He appointed McNamara head of the World Bank and named Clark Clifford, a hawk, as the new secretary of defense.

At the end of January 1968, the insurgents launched their most celebrated, concentrated offensive of the entire war. It has come to be known as the Tet Offensive, for it began on January 31, the beginning of Tet, the Vietnamese name for the lunar new year. During the week-long Confucian holiday, which the Spirit of the Hearth is believed to spend at the celestial Palace of Jade, the Vietnamese honor their ancestors. A truce had been arranged for that week. Both sides agreed that there would be no fighting.

But there was fighting—ferocious fighting. It began when Vietcong guerrillas took over the American embassy building in Saigon. At the same time, insurgents attacked nearly a hundred cities throughout South Vietnam. Weeks of carnage followed as the ARVN and American troops attempted to regain control of the cities. Many soldiers lost their lives. Many South Vietnamese civilians died too—either caught in the crossfire or butchered by the Communists.

The insurgents hoped that the Tet Offensive would spark civilian rebellions throughout South Vietnam, rebellions that would shatter the government. This did not happen. They also lost so many fighters that the cell structure in the South had to be rebuilt and restaffed by Northerners in 1969 and 1970. So in many ways Tet was a failure for them.

But Tet was in many ways a great success for them. By attacking cities for the first time, they broadened the scope of the war. No longer was the conflict confined to rural areas. All of South Vietnam—cities and villages alike—was now a battleground. The biggest benefit North Vietnam reaped from Tet was to be found in the United States. There, Americans saw on television the grisly street-fighting. They also saw what a price the United States was paying in dead and wounded. Protest became vociferous.

Shortly after Tet, General Westmoreland declared that the offensive had been a defeat for the Communists. In conventional military terms, that was an accurate assessment. Westmoreland then put in a request for 206,756 troops, most of whom would join the 525,000 American soldiers already in Vietnam.

Americans did not understand why more troops were needed in Vietnam if, as Westmoreland said, the Communists had been trounced during Tet. Secretary of Defense Clifford, having reviewed the American effort in Vietnam, had, like Robert McNamara before him, come to the conclusion that this was an unwinnable war. He began to look for ways the United States could get out.

Clifford's opinion was underscored by a group of highly respected Americans, informally dubbed the "wise men," who had once held government or military positions. First called to advise Johnson in November 1967, they had at that time supported the president in his handling of the war. The wise men were reconvened late in March 1968. By then, their views had changed dramatically. It was clear that they had been profoundly affected by Tet. Most believed that a way must be found to extricate the United States from the conflict. They agreed that the war was *perhaps* militarily winnable—in five to ten years. But they despaired of South Vietnam's ever having a government that could bind its people together and hold what was won on the battlefield.

Lyndon Johnson was snared in Vietnam. He could see no way of winning the war, and he could not bear to lose it. He had lost his support at home. Because of Vietnam, his chances of winning the 1968 election—much less the Democratic party's nomination—were slim indeed. (In his memoirs, Johnson maintains that he would have won his party's nomination and the

73

election, but he acknowledged that the American public might not have given him their support in his second term.)[9] Cornered, he stunned the nation on the evening of March 31, 1968, by announcing that he would not run again for the presidency. In the same speech, he announced a partial halt in the bombing of North Vietnam and offered to talk with the North Vietnamese. In mid-May, North Vietnamese diplomats went to Paris to meet with an American delegation headed by W. Averell Harriman. Hope that the negotiations in Paris would bring an end to the war grew even higher in October, when Johnson announced that all bombing of the North had been stopped and that representatives of the Thieu regime and the Vietcong would join the talks.

At home, the candidates vied for nomination by their parties. In the end, Hubert Humphrey, Johnson's vice-president, ran for the Democrats and Richard Nixon ran for the Republicans. Humphrey had instinctively been against the war since it began, but when he first voiced opposition to escalation at administration meetings in 1965, he had been banished from discussions for a year. The price for his inclusion in inside debates was his public support of the administration policy, and Humphrey paid that price. Not until the fall of 1968 did he wriggle free from the position of loyalty demanded by Johnson. Humphrey then campaigned with an avowal of the need for peace.

Richard Nixon also campaigned as a peace candidate. He hinted that he had a plan for obtaining peace with honor—an appealing prospect for both hawks and doves. For this reason, and because Humphrey was so closely allied to the Johnson administration and its Vietnam failure, Richard Nixon won the 1968 election by a slim margin. At the end of that year, just before Nixon took office, there were 540,000 American troops in South Vietnam.

11

President Nixon's War

Just before his inauguration as the thirty-seventh president of the United States, Richard Nixon observed that if the war continued for more than six months after the beginning of his term, it would become his war.[10]

As it turned out, the war continued for more than four years after he took office. One reason that it continued for so long was that Nixon's secret plan to get peace with honor simply did not exist.

Indeed, such a plan could not exist. The two—peace and honor—were not to be had in the same treaty. The United States and its ally, South Vietnam, were in no position to shape a peace treaty to their advantage. On the political side, the regime of Nguyen Van Thieu (pronounced Win Vahn Tee-ow), elected president in 1967, was not strong; the 1967 elections were a sham, and Thieu, like so many of his predecessors, did not command the loyalty of the South Vietnamese. On the military side, the battlefield was stalemated; the Vietcong, supplemented by regular army troops from North Vietnam, had not defeated the ARVN and American military units, but they continued to keep them on the run. Although the Vietcong and the North Vietnamese regulars had suffered vast casualties, they seemed to have no difficulty finding replacements who had the same astonishing willingness to die for the cause. A peace treaty would mean the withdrawal of American forces from South Vietnam. Nixon did not need a crystal ball to know that an American withdrawal would soon be followed by the unraveling of South Vietnam, first militarily, then politically.

North Vietnam had an advantage in having all the time in the world. The same could not be said for the United States. Opposition to the war had become strong at home. Hawks were unable to convince Americans that the war was worth it. Americans wanted their country out of the war—soon.

Given Nixon's campaign promise to gain peace with honor, the antiwar protest that had bloomed so forcefully by 1968 quieted somewhat. The negotiations, begun in Paris in May 1968, had been widened. Bombing of the North had been ended. Americans believed that a treaty was in the making. The public would give Nixon time to reach the negotiated settlement he had discussed in the 1968 campaign. Hawks trusted Nixon, an ardent anti-Communist, to get a treaty that would keep South Vietnam out of the Communist fold. Doves—at that time, mostly the young and liberals—trusted Nixon to get a treaty that would end American involvement.

But Nixon fell into the same trap that had snared Lyndon Johnson for so many years: neither wanted to be a president who lost a war. So while the Paris peace talks dragged on and on, Nixon looked for ways to ensure American withdrawal and South Vietnamese success.

Vietnamization—the process by which the burden of the war would be shifted to the ARVN—had begun during the Johnson administration. The idea was to turn the war back to what it was supposed to have been all along: South Vietnam's struggle.

Nixon continued the policy of Vietnamization, but he was not about to leave the Thieu regime entirely to the mercies of the Communists. That would signal to all the world that the United States had used a fancy name—Vietnamization—for what was in reality abandonment. To support the ARVN and the Thieu regime, Nixon decided to increase aid and bombing.

The bombing was stepped up in March 1969, and it was carried on in utter secrecy. This time the bombers were sent to Cambodia. Prince Sihanouk, head of Cambodia, had long expected the North Vietnamese to emerge as the victors. Wishing to be on the winning side, he had allowed North Vietnam to set up supply routes and bases along the Cambodian border near South Vietnam. But by late 1967 Sihanouk had begun to worry about eventually losing his own country to North Vietnam. He then told the United States that he would permit bombing of North Vietnamese sanctuaries in Cambodia.

For Nixon, bombing Cambodia offered unique possibilities. Because talks were going on in Paris with representatives from Hanoi, he could not bomb North Vietnam for fear of scuttling the negotiations. Bombing enemy sanctuaries in Cambodia was an ideal tool for Vietnamization. First, any blow to the North Vietnamese would hamper their ability to fight in the South and support the Vietcong. By incapacitating them, the United States would give the ARVN a boost in morale. So energized and less pressured by the enemy, the ARVN would be able to take on tasks previously handled by Americans and at the same time secure more territory—everyone realized that the side with the better battlefield position had the stronger hand in the peace negotiations.

That the bombing could remain secret seems incredible, but that was the case for two months. Nixon and Henry Kissinger, his national security adviser, remained silent. They were not about to announce American bombing of a neutral country, which would upset other countries around the world and infuriate the antiwar protesters at home. Sihanouk was silent too, for he was attempting to gain back American support. North Vietnam could not make the bombing public because it would at the same time be forced to acknowledge the presence of its troops in Cambodia.

When *The New York Times* first learned about and published news of the Cambodian bombing, in May 1969, the majority of Americans were not especially upset. But Nixon and Kissinger were. They were enraged that their secret had gotten out, and they wanted to know just how that had happened. They chose to tap the telephones of four journalists and thirteen government officials, a decision that would come to haunt them.

While increasing the bombing, Nixon announced in June 1969 that American troops would be gradually withdrawn from Vietnam. In one stroke, he silenced the doves, who saw in Nixon's course the beginning of disengagement, and he reassured the hawks, who were told that Vietnamization was working.

Over the previous two years, the enemy had been severely battered. In 1967, the South Vietnamese government had launched the Phoenix program. All the bits of information the ARVN and police units had gathered on Communist agents in the South were compiled, and a concerted effort was made to net the NLF. The Phoenix program provided yet another opportunity for government officials to enrich themselves. Using the threat of arrest, Phoenix agents could successfully demand what they wanted from even the loyal South Vietnamese. Agents and citizens alike used the program to settle personal disputes—a citizen's report on his or her neighbor was not always carefully checked out. As a result, many innocent civilians were arrested, tortured, or slain. Still, the program was a powerful blow to the NLF organization. Six months later, the Tet Offensive exacted another high toll on the Vietcong.

Nonetheless, the weakened Communists saw assurance of

South Vietnamese paratroopers marching into Laos

victory in Vietnamization and Nixon's announcement of troop withdrawals. The United States had lost the waiting game. As the number of Americans in South Vietnam dwindled, the Communists would at some point be able to topple the government. On September 3, 1969, a month after the first American troops left South Vietnam, Ho Chi Minh died. Although he did not live to see his country united, he must have known that his goals would be realized.

In April 1970, Nixon decided to do considerably more than bomb in Cambodia. A month earlier, Prince Sihanouk had been deposed by Lon Nol, his defense minister. Unlike Prince Sihanouk, Lon Nol was an ardent anti-Communist. To support Lon Nol's efforts to eject the Communists—both Cambodian and North Vietnamese—from his country, Nixon ordered an invasion.

American and South Vietnamese troops entered Cambodia on April 28 to attack two North Vietnamese and Vietcong bases. The bases were considerably damaged, but the North Vietnamese were quickly able to replace the weaponry. Having lost their positions in Cambodia, they simply redirected their efforts from the Mekong River delta to central Vietnam.

Although the raid was ostensibly a success and the general public was not especially aroused, the vocal elements were enraged. Nixon's right to send American troops into Cambodia, and the wisdom of that decision, were questioned, just as his right to bomb Cambodia had been questioned. At the very time that the United States was attempting to end the war in Vietnam, Nixon spread that war to another country.

The protest at home came to a crescendo that spring of 1970, sparking demonstrations across the country. In one, at Kent State University, four students were killed by National Guardsmen when the protesters stormed a reserve officers' training center. Americans were now at war with Americans.

12

Negotiations

Even before the Gulf of Tonkin incident, in 1964, government leaders around the world were trying to get Hanoi and Washington to talk. President Johnson frequently declared his interest in unconditional talks. But, in fact, he always had conditions in mind. The North Vietnamese also had conditions that had to be met before negotiations could begin. Foremost was their demand that Operation Rolling Thunder be called off. Not until 1968, when he acknowledged the futility of the Vietnam War, did Johnson curtail bombing enough to get the United States into negotiations.

The peace talks, held in Paris, were continued by President Nixon. Indeed, from the day he took office, Nixon described a treaty as the tool by which peace with honor would be achieved.

Sadly, that treaty would take four more years of wrangling. During that time the war would expand, engulfing Cambodia and Laos, and more Americans would die for Vietnam than had died during all the years before negotiations opened.

Shortly before the Cambodian invasion, in 1970, Henry Kissinger began meeting secretly in Paris with Le Duc Tho (pronounced Lay Duck Toe), the North Vietnamese who had supervised first the Vietminh effort in southern Vietnam during the war against the French, then the Vietcong effort during the American presence. Their meetings paralleled the formal negotiations, opened almost two years earlier, being carried on just a few miles away.

From the beginning, Le Duc Tho demanded what the Geneva Conference in 1954 should have produced: a solution to both the military and the political problems. He demanded an immediate removal of all American troops and a replacement of the Saigon regime with one that included members of the Vietcong. He would not go along with a proposal that North Vietnamese troops withdraw too. Le Duc Tho maintained that the Northerners were not foreigners. He defended their right to be in the South, saying that the artificial separation of their country, dating back to the Geneva agreement, was to have been temporary. In fact, North Vietnam could not afford to pull back its regular troops and leave the Vietcong to battle the ARVN, because the guerrillas were too weak to carry on on their own.

Kissinger replied that Le Duc Tho's terms were impossible. With memories of its unsavory role in the overthrow of Diem, the United States could never claim peace with honor if the agreement required it to force out what it had maintained was a legitimate government. Kissinger also saw in this demand a concern that the North Vietnamese were not strong enough to unseat Thieu on their own. Nor would Kissinger agree to a unilateral American troop withdrawal—if the United States withdrew all of its troops while North Vietnam withdrew none of its troops, the United States would obviously be forsaking its ally, South Vietnam.

Le Duc Tho and Kissinger held fast to their positions for two years. Le Duc Tho had time on his side. Kissinger did not, and this put him at a disadvantage. The unpopularity of the war at home was considerable—the Nixon administration worried

Le Duc Tho (left) und Henry Kissinger (right)

that at some point even hawks would stop supporting its Vietnam policy. In addition, American troop withdrawals were well under way, and could not easily be reversed.

With their negotiators making no headway, both sides were scrambling to improve their positions on the battlefield. As Nixon would later point out, "Successful negotiation requires the creation of conditions that make it advantageous for the other party to do what you want."[11] Early in 1971, the Nixon administration became concerned about the possibility of a Communist offensive in 1972. After all, 1972 was an election year. Many believed that the Tet Offensive, in 1968, had robbed Lyndon Johnson of a second term as president. Would the Communists use the same ploy on Nixon?

If North Vietnam was planning another concerted effort like Tet, the enemy would have to start moving matériel in 1971 before the monsoons came. American military leaders wanted to blunt such an offensive by cutting the Ho Chi Minh Trail, an ancient lacework of paths through the jungles of southern Laos and northern Cambodia, by which soldiers and supplies were filtered into South Vietnam. With Cambodia no longer available to the North Vietnamese, Laos was the key.

So plans were laid for Lamson 719, the name for a drive into Laos to strike at the Ho Chi Minh Trail. It would be carried out by the ARVN, for two reasons: first, the offensive would serve to demonstrate the success of Vietnamization; second, American troops were prohibited from entering Cambodia or Laos by congressional action taken in 1970 after the unpopular Cambodian invasion.

Both Nixon and Kissinger considered Lamson 719 a success, but others, like Stanley Karnow, a journalist, saw it as a rout. Rather than confirm the success of Vietnamization, it highlighted its failure. ARVN leaders sent half the troops American military officials thought would be needed; to make matters worse, those troops had little combat experience. Many turned back even before reaching their goal, a town twenty miles beyond the border. Many others died in fighting when they reached the town or on their retreat back to South Vietnam.

Lamson 719 had a powerful impact even beyond the battlefield. The ARVN staggered under its image as a poor fighting force—especially poor in light of the lavish training and equipment supplied by the United States since 1955. The South Vietnamese people were frightened by their army's ineffectiveness. Some expressed a resentment that the ARVN, whose casualty rate was astronomical compared with the American rate, was being asked to fight and die for American goals. There was at once a fear of America's presence and a fear of America's leaving, a sentiment that had characterized U.S.–South Vietnamese relations from the beginning, in the political, military, and economic spheres.

Although not participants in Lamson 719, American soldiers still in South Vietnam also were profoundly affected. They felt the anti-American sentiment rising in the South Vietnamese population, and they despaired that their best efforts to help South Vietnam were for naught. The lowered morale created divisiveness within the American units. Drug use was common, and units were splintered as black and white, southerner and northerner, liberal and conservative, turned against each other. In addition, men turned against their officers; there was a rise in "fragging," a process by which officers were wounded or killed when their own men threw fragmentation grenades at them. GIs did not want to be led into battle when the United States had decided to give up its role in the war.

In the United States, protesters raised their voices with renewed vigor. On June 13, 1971, *The New York Times* began publication of the so-called Pentagon Papers. Classified government documents and Defense Department analyses, the Pentagon Papers traced America's involvement in Vietnam from 1954 to 1968, showing both considerable debate about American policy within government circles and the deception of the public. Shortly after publication of the papers, both houses of Congress passed a resolution that all GIs be home by the end of 1971.

The Communist offensive that had been foreseen in 1971 began on March 30, 1972. Like Tet, it began with strikes made simultaneously throughout the country. As in Tet, the American and South Vietnamese military planners were astounded by the force of the offensive.

At that time, after massive troop withdrawals, there were 70,000 American troops in South Vietnam. Of those, only 6,000 were assigned to combat. Because of their small numbers, they were restricted in what they could do. The Thieu regime had more than a million soldiers in the ARVN, outnumbering the Communist insurgents five to one. Troops were shifted around frantically to hold first this position, then that. Because of the shifting of the ARVN forces, and because, once again, many of the ARVN units fought poorly—sometimes refusing to fight at all—the insurgents found it easy to rush in, especially in the Mekong delta. Gains in that rich region were significant. The Thieu regime was increasingly being pushed up against the wall.

The Communists paid dearly for the 1972 offensive—their casualty figures have been estimated at 50,000 dead and more than 50,000 wounded.[12] Nonetheless, they made their point. The ARVN, even with air support from the Americans, could not hold its ground. What, then, could be anticipated for the ARVN when all of the American troops were gone?

After this Communist offensive, Kissinger modified his proposal for mutual withdrawal: the United States would withdraw all its troops, while North Vietnam would withdraw only those troops sent to the South for the 1972 offensive—Northern troops in South Vietnam before then could remain. Le Duc Tho rejected the proposal, but he saw in it a shift in the American position that might signify eventual willingness to give up the whole idea of mutual withdrawal. He did give up his demand for Thieu's resignation.

In October 1972, Kissinger and Le Duc Tho arrived at an agreement. It called for a standstill cease-fire, which permitted both ARVN and Communist troops to stay in whatever territory they held at the time the peace agreement was signed; withdrawal of all American troops; and the creation of a so-called Council of Reconciliation by which the Vietnamese would resolve the political questions. Kissinger then began the process of trying to convince Thieu to accept the plan. It was important that the plan be publicly approved by the South Vietnamese government so that the United States could not be accused of abandoning the South Vietnamese.

To Thieu, the proposed agreement spelled disaster for South Vietnam. North Vietnamese troops would still be in the South. Without support from the American military, the ARVN would be overrun by the Communists. With South Vietnam's army overrun, the government would fall. Thieu wanted sixty-nine modifications to the agreement.

Kissinger felt obligated to return to Paris with Thieu's list. Le Duc Tho charged that the Americans were, in essence, proposing an entirely new agreement. In mid-December, Le Duc Tho returned to Hanoi for consultations.

Nixon was frustrated. It was imperative to get out of Vietnam, but it was also imperative to get out with self-respect. In exasperation, he turned again to bombing the North, this time the areas surrounding Hanoi and Haiphong, and he also ordered mines placed in the waters of Haiphong harbor to prevent supply ships from getting to port. Called Linebacker Two, the bombing began on December 18, 1972. For eleven days, over the Christmas holidays, American B-52s made flight after flight to drop an estimated forty-thousand tons of bombs on North Vietnam, mainly in the area between Hanoi and Haiphong.[13] The North Vietnamese sent a message to the United States that negotiations could continue when the bombing was stopped.

Kissinger and Le Duc Tho met next on January 8, 1973, and reached an agreement the day after, basically the same as that outlined the previous October. Nixon reassured Thieu that the United States would respond with force to any Communist violations of the accord. He also made clear that Thieu must go along with the agreement or go it alone.

The Paris peace accords were formally signed on January 27, 1973. The last American troops returned home from South Vietnam on March 29. Only the American diplomatic staff and civilians remained in the country. The last American prisoners of war (POWs, for short) were home from North Vietnam by April 1. With their return, the war in Vietnam came to an end for Americans—but not for the Vietnamese.

PART IV

The Vietnam War in America

Each year that it lasted Americans who took opposite sides on the war seemed to hate each other more than the Vietnamese who opposed us.

—Gloria Emerson,
Winners and Losers[1]

13

The Hawks

Hawks—those Americans who believed the United States should help the South Vietnamese wage war against the Vietcong and the North Vietnamese—offer a number of reasons for their support. All of their reasons stem from a fear of communism.

Communism is a system of government that is based on the thinking of Karl Marx, a philosopher born in Germany in 1818. The questions that he wrestled with all his life ultimately concerned economics. Looking at capitalist European societies in the mid-nineteenth century, he saw great inequity between the haves and the have-nots. The haves made up what is called the bourgeoisie, that class of people who own land or businesses. The have-nots made up what is called the proletariat, that class of people who provide the hard labor that makes the land and the businesses produce food and goods. Workers received only a minimal wage. They did not receive a share of the profits, because profits were either taken by the owner or plowed back into the business itself. The Industrial Revolution, which began about 1760, had only worsened the workers' lot. As machinery became a more important part of production, the workers became less important. They had no way to free themselves from the slavery of poverty.

Marx believed the bourgeoisie unfairly exploited the proletariat. His solution was the creation of a society in which there was no bourgeoisie. Both the means of production and the fruits of production would be shared communally. Marx knew that few members of the bourgeoisie would willingly give up their title to land or business holdings. Only by violent revolutions around the world would his new, classless society be achieved. To Marx, such a struggle seemed well worth the price, for it would bring dignity to all, not just to the powerful upper classes.

Marx's philosophy—communism—became the basis of a government when the Bolsheviks, radical members of Russia's Social Democratic Party, overthrew Czar Nicholas II in 1917. Since then, Russia—the Union of Soviet Socialist Republics, or USSR—has worked hard to extend the Communist revolution to workers around the world.

Most Westerners view the prospect of world communism with alarm. Glimpses of life in the Soviet Union and other Communist countries suggest that communism does not offer the personal dignity and democracy that Marx envisioned. The bureaucrats who manage the government, not the workers, determine what will be produced and by whom. The government, not the workers, reaps the profits. Everything—from raw materials to the workers who produce goods from those raw materials—is in service to the government's goals. For the average citizen living under communism, everyday life is studded with shortages, from food and housing to automobiles.

Communism has little regard for the citizen as an individual with individual talents, interests, and needs. But when an individual expresses opinions that are in conflict with the government's goals, that individual is seen as a threat. This is true even for artists. The composer Dmitri Shostakovich, for example, fell into disfavor because the Soviet government did not approve of his modern, dissonant music.

The governments of Communist countries go to great lengths to stifle individual expression. Information sources—newspapers, radio and television, book publishing, theaters—are closely controlled by the government. Thus the government determines what the population will and will not know. When contrary opinions still seep out, the police or the army is called in.

At the end of World War II, the Soviet Union was given responsibility for the supervision of many countries in Eastern Europe. Reneging on his promises to organize free elections in these countries, Joseph Stalin, then premier of the USSR, saw to it that Communist regimes that he could control were put in place. As the Soviet Union forced one after another of these countries into subservience, Western Europeans and Americans grew frightened. World communism was becoming a reality.

Many Americans point to the suppression of people living under communism as justification for the American war in Vietnam. To deny the individual the right to express opinions and make choices is to deny individuality and humanity—communism is by its very nature immoral. These hawks say that to stand by when others are forced into subjugation is to be guilty of neglect at the very least. As an example, they cite the millions of people put to death by the Nazis during World War II. By not acting sooner to stop that holocaust, the United States was in a way party to that immorality.

This position is held not just for idealistic reasons. Hawks point out that Communists are bent on spreading their revolution to every nation in the world. Quick to list all the countries that have come under Communist domination since World War II, many hawks embrace what is called the domino theory. Just as a row of standing dominoes will all eventually fall when the first is knocked down, capitalist democracies like our own also can be knocked down. When one country falls under Communist domination, the country next to it soon falls to Communist domination, which in turn will cause its neighbor to fall.

Now applied to situations in many areas of the world, the term *domino theory* was minted during the Indochina War. Foreseeing the French defeat at Dienbienphu, President Eisenhower warned in April 1954: "The loss of Indochina will cause the fall of Southeast Asia like a set of dominoes."[2]

In Asia, what gave the domino theory such a sharp edge was China, that massive, mysterious country pressing on Vietnam's northern border. Americans who had watched with dismay the gobbling up of Eastern European countries by the Soviets in the late 1940s were aghast to see Mao Zedong's Communist forces overcome China in 1949. When Communist Chinese troops entered the Korean War, they demonstrated a brute strength that was nothing less than frightening. Astonished by what the Chinese could do in Korea without a lavish and sophisticated arsenal, many Americans worried about what the Chinese would be able to do when they were better armed. China, these hawks maintained, must be held in check.

Hawks acknowledge that the war in Vietnam was a messy business. But they remember the lesson of Munich: by giving way to the first small demands of Nazi Germany, western Europeans set the stage for World War II. Hawks use the domino theory to point out that in going to Vietnam, we attempted to protect not only the South Vietnamese but also other countries in Southeast Asia—and, ultimately, ourselves. The journalist Marguerite Higgins summed up the implications of the domino theory:

> I believe Vietnam to be as much a front line of freedom as Hawaii or San Francisco. Perhaps more so. For if we were fighting in Hawaii or San Francisco, it might be too late.[3]

An American artillery unit preparing to fire into a suspected guerrilla area

In the process of fighting World War II, Americans had come to regard their nation's economic and military preeminence as a blessing that carried responsibilities. The United States must foster freedom and peace in the world. When small, weak nations look to the United States for assistance, the United States, with its rich, vibrant economy, can and should lend aid. For both idealistic and practical reasons, the United States, hawks assert, must lead the crusade against communism. The United States must be prepared to do more than simply set a moral example. Communism is not just an evil theory; it is an evil reality.

14
The Doves

In opposing the American war in Vietnam, doves were not expressing approval of communism—as a theory or as a reality. Like the hawks, doves are saddened by the sorry fate of all those people who have come under Communist domination. But many doves are not sure that the war in Vietnam was primarily a war against communism.

Some doves see the war as part of a longer revolution in Vietnam. It began, these doves assert, in 1941 when Ho Chi Minh organized the Vietminh to evict not one but two colonial powers. Although French colonials had dominated Vietnam for almost a hundred years, the Japanese presence was no less rankling. After the departure of the Japanese, the Vietminh fought on, for France still refused to give up its colonial claims in Vietnam.

Ours is a nation that came together by virtue of a war to expel the English, our colonial masters, more than two hundred years ago. Considering our history, most Americans would be quick to deny any desire to support or to become a colonial power. But some doves wonder if we didn't try to do both in

Vietnam. Beginning in 1950, we helped the French in their war against the Vietminh and thereby supported a colonial rule that most Vietnamese objected to. In 1956, North Vietnam could blame the United States when the elections mandated by the 1954 Geneva accords were not held. Although Diem made the decision not to hold elections, the United States, fearful of a Communist victory in the elections, applauded that decision. From the time the French left until our own diplomats had to take flight, in 1975, the United States could be seen as the one force that continued to prevent unification of the country. For twenty years, the United States's financial aid supported the existence of South Vietnam as a separate state. Americans fought alongside the ARVN. Americans served as advisers to members of the South Vietnamese government. North Vietnam referred to its enemy as "the Americans and the puppet regime of South Vietnam." There was a kernel of truth to the charge of colonialism. Exasperated American diplomats themselves often wryly referred to Diem as "a puppet who pulls his own strings."[4] Diem's successors were no more effective or pliant.

Other doves see the Vietnam War not as a revolutionary war but as a civil war between Northerners and Southerners. By reneging on the 1956 elections, the Diem regime precipitated a civil war—a conflict between groups within one country that are unable to agree or compromise on their nation's goals or leadership. While lamenting the devastation civil war brings both to a nation and to its citizens, those doves point out that foreigners should play no role in a civil war. In effect, the United States should not impose its ideas and solutions on the internal conflicts of any nation.

As the war went on, some doves recommended an American withdrawal not because they believed the war was wrong but because they believed it was unwinnable. To many people—both hawks and doves—the inability to gain victory was utterly incredible. North Vietnam was a country of about fifteen million people. Its economy was based mainly on agriculture, so it was rural. It had little industry, and no heavy industry. Its military had few armaments, and those that it had were not especially advanced. It had no air force. Still, the United States—a country of about two hundred million people, with the strongest, most diversified economy in the world and the most sophisticated technology imaginable—was unable to keep an inconsequential country like North Vietnam in line. Hawks say it was simply a question either of bringing enough might to bear or of applying that might in just the right way. Doves reply that the application of military force, including the considerable bombing in both the North and the South, was hardly restrained. Still, it did not end the war. Short of obliterating all of Vietnam, military force was an ineffective tool.

Many doves who opposed the war because it was unwinnable blame the American failure on our ally, the South Vietnamese. They point to the corruption—rigged elections; the often violent abuses of power; private profiteering, which sapped the economy—of the Diem regime and its many successors. These doves hold that it hardly mattered if the war was a war against Communist aggression, a revolutionary war, or a civil war; what mattered was that no Saigon government ever commanded the respect and loyalty of the nation as a whole. It is futile to prop up a government that its people do not want.

Many Americans opposed the war on the grounds that the United States cannot serve as policeman throughout the world. Despite our great wealth and strength, we do not have the resources to fight communism in every place that it rears its head. These doves point to Western Europe, Israel, and Japan as our most important allies. Distracted by Vietnam, we had little time to consider their pressing concerns, and our armed forces stationed in other parts of the world were spread dangerously thin.

Other doves believe that American policymakers were working on outdated assumptions about the nature of communism. George Kennan, a longtime student of American foreign policy, pointed out in 1967 that unity within the Communist bloc was a thing of the past. Every country has its own overriding national interest. While Americans in the 1950s and early 1960s often imagined that one policy line was handed down from Moscow and that all other members of the Communist bloc toed that line, such was not the case.[5] That idea was most emphatically demonstrated by what has come to be called the Sino-Soviet split, an uneasiness between China and the Soviet Union dating back to the late 1950s. So serious is their difference of opinion that both nations still mass a large proportion of their armies along their common border. The American war in Vietnam provided the one issue on which they agreed. Despite their rift, both the Soviet Union and China joined forces to supply aid to North Vietnam. When the war ended, the Soviet Union and China began competing against each other in Laos and Cambodia.

Bernard Fall was one who also believed that nationalism is a strong force even in Communist countries. He suggested that if the United States feared that the Chinese would take over Indochina and then all the rest of Southeast Asia, then the United States should support *North* Vietnam. Vietnam had a firm, age-old hatred of Chinese domination, and the North Vietnamese had demonstrated the will and the ability to get foreigners out.[6]

Kennan pointed out not only that various Communist countries have their own particular interests but also that communism has undergone many changes and is still changing.[7] By the mid-1960s, Communists saw benefits in working with capitalists. At the same time Americans were killing and being killed by Vietcong guerrillas and North Vietnamese soldiers, American diplomats were drawing up agreements for trade, cultural exchanges, and limitations on nuclear weapons with the Soviets. In the early 1970s, Americans enthusiastically welcomed President Nixon's diplomatic opening to China.

U.S. marines waiting to advance in the rubble of the citadel of Hue during the Tet Offensive

Finally, there are doves who opposed the war because of the way it was conducted. Bombs, defoliants, and napalm (a jellylike substance in weapons such as firebombs that sticks to human flesh and causes prolonged burning) were used extensively. The various pacification programs, programs meant to protect and win over the South Vietnamese, created millions of refugees. In protecting the South Vietnamese from communism, these doves argued, we took away their livelihood if not their lives. A famous, telling comment on what the war did to our allies was made during the Tet Offensive: describing the battle for Bentre, an American military officer said, "We had to destroy the town to save it."[8]

15
The Media

Americans disagreed not only about whether the United States should be waging war in Vietnam but also about how the war was going. It was often difficult to grasp even the day-to-day reality of Vietnam. Yet never before had the media offered Americans at home such a wealth of facts, descriptions, and photographs.

In the beginning, the American public hardly knew there was a war. Although the United States had been supporting South Vietnam since 1954, even the media were slow to pay attention to this Asian ally. The 1960 coup attempt by South Vietnamese army units piqued the interest of *The New York Times*, which sent Homer Bigart to Saigon. He joined a small band of other correspondents who struggled to find out just what was going on.

The correspondents then in South Vietnam struggled on two fronts. Ngo Dinh Diem was especially prickly about reporters' criticism of his regime and its efforts to put down the Vietcong guerrillas. Having hushed criticism in South Vietnam, he was anxious to hush criticism in the United States. After all, bad news about South Vietnam might make the Americans reconsider their commitment. Diem knew he could not do without American aid.

The Diem regime had ways to curb correspondents. It could, and did, accuse them of being Communists. It could, and did, refuse to talk to reporters. But its most powerful weapon was to withdraw a reporter's visa permitting him or her to be in South Vietnam.

In 1962, Diem attempted to expel two foreign correspondents, Homer Bigart and François Sully, a Frenchman whose articles appeared in *Newsweek* magazine. Only because of pressure from American officials in Saigon did the Diem regime relent and allow them to stay. (The regime later succeeded in expelling Sully.)

The high American officials in Saigon who had intervened on that occasion were also prickly about news coverage. They had two problems. First, they were trying desperately to conceal American military advisers' involvement in actual fighting with the Vietcong. The advisers were, in fact, much more than mere advisers, and that might not sit well with the American public.

Second, the American officials, well aware of the faults of the Diem regime and its army, feared that criticism would provoke Diem to sever his ties with the United States. Then the United States would lose this opportunity to battle communism. While officials in Saigon were working hard to convince reporters that things were going well in South Vietnam, Kennedy administration officials in Washington were also working hard to keep the media in the dark. At one point, McGeorge Bundy, national security adviser to Presidents Kennedy and Johnson, summed up the government's approach to the media: "A communiqué should say nothing, in such a way as to fool the press without deceiving them."[9]

Reporters in Saigon knew that they were being deceived. There American military officials held daily press briefings in the late afternoon. Forced optimism and evasiveness were chronic, and before long, the press corps came to refer to the briefings as the "five-o'clock follies." So the correspondents turned to other sources in South Vietnam.

Their counterparts at home had no such alternative. As a consequence, newspaper and television editors found the information from their reporters in Saigon very different from the information supplied by various government sources in Washington. So different was the news from Saigon and the news from Washington that editors had to choose one or the other. Early in the war, they tended to go with the information from Washington. Their decision was reinforced by John Mecklin, a newsman hired by the State Department to sort out what had come to be called the press mess. Mecklin reported that, in his opinion, the correspondents in Saigon were inexperienced and that their reports were unnecessarily pessimistic.

Even the most experienced correspondents in Saigon had difficulties with their editors at home. So many of Charles Mohr's articles for *Time* magazine were turned inside out that he quit early in 1964. For a long while after that, *Time* continued to reflect the optimism of government officials in Washington. David Halberstam later mused on why this happened:

> Part of the reason for this, I think, was because of the particular way in which *Time*'s executives view the magazine: to a large degree they see it not just as a magazine of reporting, but as an instrument of policy making. Thus, what *Time*'s editors *want* to happen is as important as what is happening.[10]

Still, some correspondents succeeded in getting their analyses to the public. Halberstam, then a correspondent for *The New York Times*, was one. Seeing that the efforts of government officials in both Saigon and Washington had not prevented the gloomier reports from getting out, President Kennedy himself complained to the *Times*. He asked that Halberstam be reassigned. The *Times* said no.[11]

As the Vietcong stepped up their guerrilla attacks and discord in Saigon grew, the press corps expanded. At the height of the war, there were more than six hundred correspondents in South Vietnam from news organizations around the world. Despite the extraordinary risks many in this army of correspondents took to gather masses of information, some students of the Vietnam War think that the American public was not well informed. Phillip Knightley, a newsman who has written on war reportage, believes that one reason the public was not well informed was because the correspondents were addressing only half of the problem—"the correspondents were not questioning the American intervention itself but only its effectiveness."[12] The American dilemma had, from the start, two sides: the purpose behind this war and the way to win this war. Early on, many correspondents saw that the war was not going well, but they rarely asked why Americans had gone to South Vietnam in the first place.

The public was also not well informed because the media, as the messenger of bad news, came to be as unwelcome as the bad news itself. Harrison Salisbury, of *The New York Times*, visited Hanoi in 1966. Upon his return, he wrote articles reporting the bombing of civilian targets. The Johnson administration was enraged. It had all along maintained that the air strikes were targeted for military installations and that no civilians were harmed. Further, the administration had assured the American public that the technology of air strikes was so advanced that there could be no errors. Salisbury's articles left the administration with an unpalatable choice. It could admit that it could not always vouch for the accuracy of the bombers and that, sadly, on some occasions civilians were hurt. Or the administration could defend the accuracy of its bombers; in that case, it would have to

A father with the body of his child, killed when ARVN forces pursued Vietcong guerrillas into a village. Photographs like this won Horst Faas a Pulitzer Prize.

acknowledge that it was targeting civilian areas. Either way, the administration had to deal with a "credibility gap"—a discrepancy between what it said it was doing and what it did.[13] The Pentagon responded by ignoring the real issue and referring to Salisbury as "Ho Chi Salisbury of the *Hanoi Times*."[14]

Having come late to the story in Vietnam, the media also left early. According to Knightley, from 1969 on, many news organizations turned their attention to the negotiations in Paris. As a consequence, they gave less coverage to what was happening in Vietnam. In addition, those correspondents who remained in South Vietnam after the Paris peace talks opened found American officials in Saigon more guarded than ever. It is easy to see why. The war was intensifying. In an effort to improve their negotiating positions, both sides were fighting ferociously to gain and hold territory. More important, the secret bombing of Cambodia had begun, and the military was intent on keeping it a secret.

Those who question just how well informed the American public was also look to the role of television. Most of the American public gets its news from television. Yet news broadcasts are made up of short segments covering a multitude of events taking place all over the world. Given its extraordinary complexity, the Vietnam War could not be well analyzed during a standard news program.

Still, if television did not explain the war, most people assume that it turned many Americans against the war. Every night, Americans saw film clips of the carnage. If they were not actual participants, they were nonetheless observers, a role that Americans at home had not played in previous wars. Television, many maintain, gave rise to an overwhelming revulsion from war.

Some thoughtful students of television disagree. Michael Arlen, writing in *The New Yorker*, suggested that television in fact heightened the unreality of the war:

I can't say I completely agree with people who think that when battle scenes are brought into the living room the hazards of war are necessarily made "real" to the civilian audience. It seems to me that by the same process they are also made less "real"—diminished, in part, by the physical size of the television screen, which, for all the industry's advances, still shows one a picture of men three inches tall shooting at other men three inches tall, and trivialized, or at least tamed, by the cozy alarums of the household.[15]

Yet another problem with televised war reportage comes from the American public's love of war movies, movies that had made up a sizable proportion of their viewing diet for years before the war. Michael Herr, a Vietnam war correspondent, spoke of "our movie-fed war fantasies."[16] Images flickering on the evening news may well have been confused by many Americans with a war movie whose plot was particularly murky.

Blaming the media for turning Americans at home against the war, one officer lashed out at correspondents: "My Marines are winning this war and you people are losing it for us in your papers."[17] Stanley Karnow thinks that isn't so—"the press, with all its shortcomings, tended to follow rather than lead the U.S. public."[18] But if the media did not shape public opinion, they certainly provoked it. Whether the coverage was accurate, the focus correct, or even if a great deal of information was concealed from the media, the war was brought home to the people. And for a variety of reasons—intellectual disapproval, emotional disgust, exhaustion, even boredom—Americans forced their government to withdraw from the war.

16

Protest at Home

Protest against the war was late and slow in developing. It developed late because for a long time the American public was hardly aware that American military personnel were in South Vietnam. And once they learned about that, the public was for a long time unaware just how deeply U.S. military personnel were actually involved in the conflict.

Even in March 1965, when the first combat troops landed in South Vietnam, few Americans were deeply concerned. After all, only 3,500 marines were sent, and their only role was to protect the American air base at Danang.

Nine months later, nearly 200,000 American troops were in Vietnam, and their role had expanded greatly to include the hazardous search-and-destroy missions. By then, many Americans began to wonder about the appropriateness of their involvement.

Protest developed slowly because it originated with the young. The first people who looked at the war in Vietnam most critically were male high school and college students. With the selective-service draft in effect, many would be off to the military as soon as diplomas or degrees were handed out.

Many young men decided that the war in Vietnam was not for them. Some regarded all war as immoral. Many others were not willing to serve in this war, a war that seemed incomprehensible despite the abundance of information brought home by the media. Many simply did not want to risk their lives for their country, no matter what the conflict.

Those who believe that all war is immoral are called conscientious objectors. The government recognizes conscientious objection, and draft regulations provided for alternative service—for example, work in a hospital—for those who could prove their deep religious or moral aversion to war.

Those whose unwillingness to join the military could not be attributed to religious or moral scruples had to find other ways out. The draft system permitted college and graduate-school students postponements, or deferments. Many young men enrolled for higher education. They hoped the war would sputter to an end by the time their next graduation ceremonies were at hand. By the beginning of 1968, colleges and universities were not safe havens. Draft regulations were changed so that deferments no longer could be obtained by graduate students; the year had opened with almost half a million American troops in Vietnam; at the end of January, the ferocious Tet Offensive began. The war was clearly not going to end soon.

Unhappy about what military service might mean to their lives, many men nonetheless complied with the draft and were inducted into the armed forces. Others, called draft dodgers, looked for one way or another to avoid serving. For some draft dodgers, employment was a way out. Jobs with companies that make military equipment meant exemptions, as did jobs in teaching. Others married and quickly had children, because all men who were fathers, except doctors and dentists, were excused from military service. Still other draft dodgers left the United States, knowing they could not set foot again on American soil without risking arrest.

Yet another way of draft-dodging was to fail the physical

examination. James Fallows, as a senior at Harvard University, employed this approach by dieting until he weighed 120 pounds—not much for a six-foot one-inch man.

At the time, Fallows believed that his action would help end the war. If the draft could not supply the military with enough men, the United States could not wage war in Vietnam. He recalled a talk antiwar activist Michael Ferber gave to Harvard students:

> Did we realize that the draft machine was tottering towards its ultimate breakdown? . . . That each body we withheld from its ravenous appetite brought it that much nearer the end?[19]

Fallows subsequently wrestled with the moral questions posed by draft-dodging. Some 26.8 million American men came of age between mid-1964 and early 1973. Of those, about 11 million served in the military. Three million served in Vietnam. Nearly 16 million men provided no military service whatsoever.[20] Fallows came to recognize that the draft never failed to find the people it needed. For all the men who could find a way around the draft, there were others who were netted.

Who went? Statistics show that the people who went into the military and off to Vietnam tended to be those who could not afford a college education, those who could not find jobs in professions that provided exemptions, or those who had no connections with the people in power who could pull strings. Disturbed by the unfairness of the draft system, Fallows came to believe that this unfairness was in large measure responsible for the length of the war:

> Because the upper class didn't send kids to war, they didn't oppose it in something other than a bloodless way. . . . The more the burden of the war was shifted on families who had the least influence, the longer the war went on.[21]

*An anti-antiwar demonstrator with a placard alluding to the
Buddhist self-immolations*

Once they found a way around the draft, many dodgers went back to their own lives. Even though the Vietnam War still raged, it was no longer a problem for them. Only a few felt a need to make a moral stand on the war. Some left the United States not just to evade the draft but to show their disapproval of America's involvement in what they thought was an immoral war. Some refused to serve in the military and served prison terms instead. Some, like Samuel Brown, spent the remaining war years trying to mobilize public opinion against the war.

Because of what it might mean to them, students took the lead in demonstrating against the war. Colleges and universities were frequent scenes of marches, sit-ins, antiwar speeches, and draft-card burnings. Antiwar and anti-antiwar demonstrators hurled insults at each other. In November 1965, Americans were horrified by the self-immolation of two youths, one in front of the Pentagon and the next, a few days later, in front of the United Nations.

But beyond the young, the public as a whole was slow to join the protest movement. Today many wonder if, ironically, America's passionate young hindered the development of broad antiwar sentiment. The historian Barbara Tuchman says: "Because protest was associated in the public mind with drugs and long hair and the counterculture of the decade, it may have slowed rather than stimulated general dissent." Of the 1965 self-immolations, she points out that to Americans, the act seemed "too crazed to influence the American public, except maybe negatively, as equating antiwar protests in the public mind with emotional misfits."[22]

Many older Americans were appalled by the behavior of the young. It seemed to them that patriotism had suddenly, silently died. Veterans of World War II and the Korean War, proud of their service and of American involvement in those wars, were bitter; the United States, a country that had given its young so much, would not be defended by the young.

Tensions in American society did not arise only between the

young and the old. Proportionately many more blacks and less advantaged Americans than privileged whites found themselves in the military—and in Vietnam. Blacks resented whites; the poor resented the rich.

Government officials, especially in the Nixon administration, came to see protest not as one of Americans' most profound rights but as a willful effort to destroy the government. Indeed, horrified by the sea of 250,000 demonstrators at a 1969 rally in Washington, Attorney General John Mitchell said, "It looked like the Russian Revolution."[23]

Despite the tensions that rent the American public, the antiwar movement did gradually expand to embrace more than just the young. The movement also came to embrace more than just the doves. Many Americans who turned against the Vietnam War did so not because they believed the reasons we were in South Vietnam were wrong. Nor were they disturbed by our methods of war—in fact, many of these Americans believed that the military was not being aggressive enough, and some even advocated the use of nuclear weapons against North Vietnam. Nor did they always see the casualty figures as unacceptably high. They turned against the war because it was costing too much, both financially and emotionally. The government was attempting to wage war abroad without adjusting the economy at home, a tactic that was proven unworkable by 1967, when there was a federal deficit of $9.8 billion. Taxes were increased, but the financial outpouring seemed to accomplish nothing. The war in Vietnam was still not being won. More Americans—sons and boyfriends and next-door neighbors—were dying, and for what? At the same time, the war at home was getting worse. With the government unable to break the military stalemate in Vietnam and unable to bind together its citizenry at home, many Americans who were neither young nor doves finally bowed to the sheer futility of the war.

PART V

After
the Battle

Was the war we fought ... morally worse than Communism itself?

—*Norman Podhoretz,*
Why We Were in
Vietnam[1]

17

The Communist Victory

For Americans, the Vietnam War came to an end in 1973. All combat troops were home by April, although members of the Nixon administration warned that they might be sent back if the truce was violated by the Communists. Sick of the war, Congress passed legislation prohibiting any more expenditure of funds for U.S. military operations anywhere in Indochina. This ensured that, despite what might happen, U.S. troops would under no circumstances return to the Vietnamese battlefield. It also put an end to the bombing of Communist sanctuaries in Cambodia, which had not been covered by the Paris peace accords and had thus been continued.

According to Stanley Karnow:

> Thieu's regime was in relatively sturdy shape at the start of the truce. His army, equipped with last-minute deliveries of American weapons and still receiving U.S. aid, controlled roughly 75 percent of South Vietnam's territory and about 85 percent of its population.[2]

When his allies departed, Thieu set about to gain complete control. While his regime worked to silence dissent, his army worked to extend control over all of the South and its people.

In contrast, the Communists were weak. The Phoenix program, Tet, and, most recently, the 1972 offensive, all had severely depleted their ranks of guerrilla fighters and seasoned North Vietnamese army regulars. But as Henry Kissinger later pointed out, "It is a cardinal principle of guerrilla warfare that the guerrilla wins if he does not lose; the regular army loses unless it wins."[3]

The Hanoi leadership decided to lie low, endorsing confrontations with the ARVN only in those instances when the insurgents had a clear advantage. All the while, however, North Vietnamese soldiers were infiltrated into the South—a violation of the Paris peace agreement.

In 1974, General Tran Van Tra (pronouned Trahn Vahn Trah), a Communist commander positioned in the South, devised a military plan by which the final takeover of the South would be effected. He believed it could be completed in 1976. But late in 1974, the Communist leaders in Hanoi thought the plan too bold. They endorsed only the first step, the taking of Phuoclong Province, north of Saigon. And they would not commit the number of troops Tran Van Tra requested. Nevertheless, the province fell to the Communists on January 6, 1975. With that victory, the Hanoi leadership decided to step up its pace. The next objective was Banmethuot. That too was taken, on March 10, 1975.

Seeing that the ARVN was piece by piece being overcome by the Communist forces, Thieu began evacuating the northern area of South Vietnam. With ARVN troops taking flight, followed by frightened Southern civilians, the Communists found less resistance than they had anticipated. They also found that they would have to move up their timetable and hurry to take Saigon, the prize. If they postponed the taking of the capital until after the monsoon season, the Thieu regime might use that time to rebuild its strength.

The Communist rush to Saigon was slowed at Xuanloc, where the ARVN held off the insurgents for two weeks. But the

Communists broke through on April 21. Only then did the American embassy put final evacuation procedures into motion.

Concerned about causing panic and convinced that Saigon could be withheld from the Communists' grasp, Graham Martin, then U.S. ambassador to South Vietnam, had delayed evacuation. Late in getting under way, the evacuation was extraordinarily complex. It involved not only American citizens who remained in Vietnam but also South Vietnamese citizens who had worked so closely with the Americans that their lives would be in jeopardy if the Communists came to power.

All told, more than fifty thousand Americans and South Vietnamese were taken out of the country. Seven thousand of those left in the eighteen hours just before the Communist insurgents arrived in Saigon. Having watched the televised horror of the battlefield for so many years, Americans watched the televised horror of the evacuation on April 30, 1975. For every South Vietnamese who made the evacuation list, there were many more—low-level government workers and ARVN soldiers—who did not. Many Americans feared that the Communists would unleash a bloodbath, so the sight of desperate South Vietnamese being pushed from the helicopters—and safety—was searing.

The transfer of power from the Saigon regime to the Communists took place on the morning of April 30 in the presidential palace. Saigon was renamed Ho Chi Minh City, and the Communists took control with little difficulty. Foreigners who remained in the country after the departure of the last Americans noted that most of the South Vietnamese population was neither elated nor frightened by the Communist takeover. By late fall 1975, armed resistance to the Communists was limited to small groups in remote areas. One and a half million people were sent to "reeducation" camps, where they were told the dos and don'ts of life under communism. Many were soon released, but thousands are still there. The Communists were especially suspicious of educated Southerners. By imprisoning them, the new leaders imprisoned the very people who might have made rebuilding the country easier.

North and South Vietnam were not immediately united. The Communists preferred first to try to stabilize the South. The economy was in a shambles. Joblessness had started to rise early in the war when peasants, displaced by bombing in the rural areas, had moved to the cities. There many eked out their living as cooks, prostitutes, or vendors of black-market goods to the vast numbers of Americans connected with the war. After the U.S. troops left in 1973, the Thieu regime could offer no real work, and cities swarmed with even more beggars than before.

To solve the problems of unemployment and a shortage of food, the Communist regime opened what are called New Economic Areas (NEAs). Set up mostly along Vietnam's western border, the New Economic Areas are farming areas devised to offer employment for the refugees and expanded food supplies for the nation. But not until 1982 could Vietnam get along without food imports.

Some businesses belonging to foreigners and all banks were immediately seized. Fearful of killing what little life was in the economy and anxious not to antagonize the Southerners, the Communist regime waited to take over, or nationalize, private enterprise. Nationalization of trade and collectivization of land did not begin until 1978. So far, collectivization has not worked in the rich Mekong delta. It is estimated that only 20 percent of the rice farmers belong to the collectives.[4]

It was nationalization of trade that brought Vietnam once again into world headlines. Beginning in 1978, when the Communist regime started nationalizing small businesses, there was a mass exodus. The people trying to leave Vietnam came to be called the boat people, for they fled by sea on barges or junks— whatever they could get on. An estimated one million Vietnamese—mostly ethnic Chinese, who made up the vast majority of small businessmen, but also some Vietnamese unhappy under communism—have tried to leave.[5] Escaping in frail, unseawor-

Vietnamese boat people denied permission to leave the cargo hold
of the freighter on which they escaped to the Philippines

thy boats, many drowned. Others were murdered at sea by pirates. Many of those who survived found themselves turned away and towed back to sea by ships of the Asian countries where they landed. To help the Vietnamese refugees, many nations, including the United States, raised their immigration quotas for them. Even so, hundreds of thousands of the refugees remain in squalid refugee centers waiting for relocation.

The Communist regime has not been able to rid Vietnam of the French and American influences prevalent before the fall of South Vietnam. Even Communist officials have developed a taste for those possessions the Communist leadership finds so threatening. When an official acquires a cassette tape player and plays it at high volume, the leadership worries about his "revolutionary purity"—his single-minded commitment to the cause. The corruption that was so widespread in South Vietnam also continues to flourish. Indeed, it has spread to the once puritanical northern half of the country. Throughout the country, the black market booms. Bribery of government officials is common. Even the state-controlled press has acknowledged signs of corruption and laziness in the military.

Vietnam—formally the Socialist Republic of Vietnam since 1976—has also had difficulties in its foreign relations. It has warred with both Cambodia and China. Efforts by President Carter's administration to establish diplomatic ties did not succeed. The Hanoi leadership demanded $3.2 billion they say President Nixon secretly promised during the Paris peace negotiations. The Carter administration said it was doubtful that this would be approved by Congress. By the time Hanoi dropped the demand, Washington had lost interest in diplomatic relations. Relations with China were more important.

In light of the problems Vietnam has within and outside its borders, it is not surprising that Prime Minister Pham Van Dong (pronounced Fahm Vahn Dong), who headed the Vietminh delegation at the 1954 Geneva Conference, should observe, "Waging a war is simple, but running a country is very difficult."[6]

18

Vets at Home

In 1980, a Harris poll found most Americans have high regard for veterans of the Vietnam War.[7] But upon their return home during and at the end of the American military involvement in South Vietnam, many veterans felt themselves unwelcome. Some were quietly shunned or even openly scorned by their neighbors.

The hostility some American civilians felt toward Vietnam veterans may have grown out of the realization that the United States had lost the war—despite President Nixon's assurances that the Paris peace accords had brought us "peace with honor." A man who had worked for the U.S. military mission in the early 1960s observed, "I'm ashamed we got beaten so badly."[8] Many Americans felt just the same way. Frustrated, they sometimes vented their feelings on individual veterans. Veterans were not just the easiest mark; they were the only mark. The Vietcong and North Vietnamese were far away, in Asia, as were our allies, the South Vietnamese. The thousands of U.S. government bureaucrats who made the countless decisions that ultimately brought America to defeat were a faceless mass in Washington.

Other Americans were not so much concerned about defeat

as about the immorality of war in general and this war in particular. They looked at the returning veterans as symbols of that immorality. Tim Page, a Vietnam War correspondent, has said:

> War has always been glamorous. And I don't care who he is, if you put a gun in a man's hand, then he feels bigger.[9]

Such sentiments make many people wonder how often wars have been waged not for causes but to satisfy a dark need of human nature. As the technology of war becomes more sophisticated and widespread, that question becomes all the more urgent.

Many Americans were deeply disturbed by the nature of our weaponry. Napalm was not invented for the Vietnam War, but its use there was extensive. Some consider napalm utterly inhumane, the weapon of an evil army that relishes the slow, ghastly burning of human flesh. Defoliants have contaminated much of South Vietnam's rich farmland. One, the defoliant Agent Orange, has been blamed for the high rate of cancer experienced by Vietnam veterans.

The Vietnam War was also filled with atrocities, acts of brutality that go far beyond the limits of human behavior, even in war. Americans always knew that Communists commit atrocities—indeed, that is one of the reasons we have fought communism. But Americans have a hard time imagining that their own troops could be so barbarous.

Perhaps the most widely known incident was the Mylai massacre, which took place on March 16, 1968. The statistics for a skirmish with the Vietcong there are as follows:

> Killed in action: 128 Vietcong
> Captured in action: 11 Vietcong
> Weapons captured: 3 rifles

That 139 Vietcong had only three rifles suggested that some-

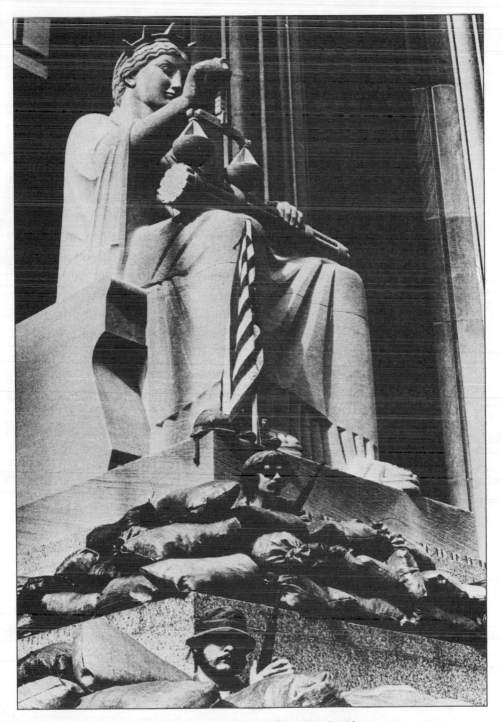

Two members of Vietnam Veterans Against the War armed with toy rifles at the Federal Courthouse in St. Louis to demonstrate their support for Vietnam veterans accused of conspiring to disrupt the 1972 Republican National Convention

thing was wrong with the numbers. In fact, more than a hundred civilians had been massacred.

Ronald Ridenhour, a vet who had heard murmurs of Mylai during his year of service in Vietnam, pressed for an investigation. The U.S. military reluctantly scheduled courts-martial, or military trials.

None of this became public until Seymour Hersh, a reporter for *The New York Times*, stumbled across a small announcement of the court-martial of Lieutenant William Calley at Fort Benning, Georgia, in November 1970. With public scrutiny of the Calley court-martial and that of Captain Ernest Medina, in September 1971, Americans belatedly came to recognize that Americans themselves are not above committing atrocities. Many were caught in conflicting emotions: they wrestled with moral indignation against reprehensible acts committed in the name of the United States; yet they recognized that in a guerrilla war, those who seem to be civilians are not always so—the woman carrying a baby might also be carrying a grenade.

Americans also sensed that the publicity surrounding Mylai represented only the tip of the iceberg. Phillip Knightley agrees:

> The word "atrocity" requires careful handling, but it can be argued that My Lai was *not* an atrocity—at least if it is argued that an atrocity is taken to be something freakish, something quite apart from the normal events coming before and after it. My Lai, on the contrary, was an unusually pure example of the nature of the war in Vietnam and departed little—if at all—from common American practice.[10]

Late in the war, Americans also began to hear about other unsavory aspects of the U.S. presence in Vietnam. There was a growing population of young children fathered by American soldiers, then left behind with no support when their fathers' tours of duty in Vietnam were over. These children were, and still are, treated as outcasts by the Vietnamese.

In addition, Americans began to hear about the staggering toll taken by drugs, so easily available to American soldiers in Vietnam. Official military reports in 1971 acknowledged that use of marijuana was common. Further, it was estimated that close to a third of the American troops used opium or heroin.[11]

National defeat, demonic weapons, atrocities, abandoned children, mind-blowing drugs—these were aspects of the Vietnam War not at all in line with American values. Unable to reconcile the United States's experience in Vietnam with those values, Americans often exploded in angry outbursts or withdrew into silence. Their treatment of veterans of that war was an expression of emotional paralysis.

Many, many veterans returned from Vietnam with severe physical problems—a much higher percentage than in previous wars. Some blame this on the one-year tour of duty. Casualty figures were much higher for soldiers newly arrived in Vietnam; just when they had learned how to stay alive in a guerrilla war, they were sent home, their tour in Vietnam over. Then too, many soldiers who would have died in an earlier war survived the Vietnam War because of the speedy delivery of excellent medical treatment. But their injuries were extensive, and if these veterans were not permanently disabled, they would nonetheless require long and arduous rehabilitation and physical therapy.

Emotional distress also was more common for veterans of the Vietnam War. Many came home with what has been called Post-Vietnam Syndrome—PVS, for short. All wars produce psychological problems. Only the names change. In World War I, people spoke of "shell shock." In World War II, they called it "battle fatigue." The high rate of PVS is often linked to the average age of soldiers—nineteen in Vietnam. (The average World War II soldier was twenty-six.)[12] Then, to some degree, PVS can be attributed to the way the war was managed. Soldiers went to Vietnam not in units but one by one, to be plugged in to existing units as replacements. This gave rise to a sense of lonely isolation for individual soldiers. When they came home, they were whisked by jets that allowed no opportunity for unwinding. The slow troop ships bringing American forces home after World War II had offered them the time to work through among themselves their emotions and experience.

The nature of a guerrilla war added to the emotional stress that plagued Vietnam veterans. The Vietnam War was a war without military fronts; a war mostly of hit-and-run skirmishes and sniper attacks instead of classic, conventional battles; a war against enemies not in uniform. Very few places in South Vietnam were safe, even for troops not out on patrols. This constant danger and fear can have lasting effects.

The federal government has provided less assistance than might be expected. In the fall of 1972, President Nixon vetoed the Veterans' Medical Care Expansion Act, saying that it was inflationary. Benefits for Vietnam veterans under the GI Bill of Rights are much less than the benefits veterans of World War II received.

Home again, Vietnam veterans have had a hard time putting the war into their past. Few Americans at home provided a sympathetic ear for veterans who needed to relate their experiences. Even those veterans who were physically and emotionally able found it hard to get going again. Applying to law school, one veteran, Dean Phillips, encountered difficulties with a three-member selection committee; one professor wanted no veterans admitted.[13] Like the war in Vietnam, the war in America did not end with the signing of the Paris peace accords.

19

The Weakened Giant

Along with many of its veterans, the United States as a nation was wounded by the Vietnam War. Some of the nation's wounds have yet to heal.

Damage to the military was visible by the early 1970s. David Halberstam believes that the professional officers corps was especially harmed. Those officers who challenged the wisdom of established policy frequently lost promotions. Seeing their careers at a standstill, many quit in disgust.[14]

The quality of combat troops also fell after the war. The draft was ended at the same time the Paris peace accords were signed. Not surprisingly, the people who joined the military after such an unpopular war had little education and few employment prospects. Recently, however, young adults have shown renewed interest in military careers, and swelling numbers of applicants have allowed all branches of the armed services to be increasingly selective.

Unlike our military, our damaged economy is not recovering. Traditionally, when a country goes to war, it adjusts its economy accordingly. During World War II, for example, people at home were encouraged to plant "victory gardens" to grow their own vegetables. Other commodities, from cloth to fuel, were rationed. War is expensive—the total cost of the Vietnam War has been estimated at $165 billion.[15] One reason President Johnson shied away from a formal declaration of war was his fear that Congress would then refuse to pass his expensive social legislation.

He had the war and his Great Society program, but it didn't work. In 1967, the first deficit in the federal budget appeared. The cost of the war in 1968 alone was $27 billion; the deficit for that year alone was $23 billion.[16] The deficit for 1986 is expected to be $200 billion.[17] The successive years of mushrooming deficits have contributed to periods of high unemployment, high interest rates, and recession. The prospect of a balanced budget is many years off.

But perhaps the greatest wound to the nation is the distrust that has grown up between Americans and their government. John Kennedy, Lyndon Johnson, Richard Nixon—all three presidents carefully orchestrated information about what the United States was doing in Vietnam. Each in his own way mounted what was in effect a public-relations campaign, glossing over military advisers who were really fighting, the true facts in the Gulf of Tonkin incident, the Cambodian bombing. There is even reason to doubt what the three presidents claimed was our goal in Vietnam. In March 1965, one month after the start of Operation Rolling Thunder, Defense Department aide John McNaughton summarized American aims:

70%—To avoid a humiliating U.S. defeat (to our reputation as a guarantor).
20%—To keep SVN (and the adjacent) territory from Chinese hands.
10%—To permit the people of SVN to enjoy a better, freer way of life.

ALSO—To emerge from crisis without unacceptable
taint from methods used.

NOT—to "help a friend," although it would be hard to
stay in if asked out.[18]

American prestige, not South Vietnam, was what was at stake.

Both President Johnson and President Nixon were caught
in Vietnam. For Johnson, the unpopularity of the war forced him
to withdraw from the 1968 campaign for his party's nomination.
Senator Eugene McCarthy campaigned for convention dele-
gates on an antiwar platform. His fine showing in the New
Hampshire primary proved that Democrats were not united
behind their party's policy on Vietnam. With Robert Kennedy's
entry into the race, Johnson faced a truly powerful antiwar
competitor. Johnson withdrew because his ability to hold even
his own party's support was questionable.

Some activities that led up to Nixon's resignation grew out
of the Vietnam War. His constitutional right to bomb Cambodia
was questioned. Dissent by leading members of Congress and
by well-known writers provoked Nixon to draw up his "enemies
list." The publication of the Pentagon Papers in June 1971 so
angered Nixon that shady figures in the employ of his campaign
organization set out to discredit Daniel Ellsberg, the former
State Department employee who had given the classified documents to the press. They broke into the office of Ellsberg's
psychiatrist. Perhaps something would be found there with
which to discredit Ellsberg.

The articles of impeachment against President Nixon did
not refer to the Vietnam War. But the disrespect for both American citizens and American law that is at the heart of the Water-
gate break-in was merely one more expression of the values that
characterized Nixon's response to antiwar opposition. Nixon's
resignation put a dark blot on his own reputation. In addition, it
put a dark blot on the presidency itself. Dubious about the

candor and wisdom of the Kennedy and Johnson administrations, many Americans saw Nixon's resignation as crowning
proof that presidents are not to be trusted.

Americans' suspiciousness about the people who run their
government did not ebb when Nixon left office. Samuel Brown,
who worked for so many years as an antiwar activist, observes:

> No country can long survive if a significant portion of its
> citizens are unwilling to sanction the action of its leaders.
>
> How those in power come to terms with the issue of
> restoring that trust seems to me to be a critical issue of the
> 1980s. I see no indication that those now in power in Wash-
> ington have any understanding of how to go about regaining
> that trust.[19]

The Vietnam War also profoundly affected American standing with other nations. U.S. policy in Vietnam often appeared
not at all in harmony with the nation's professed high ideals.
Ultimately, actions speak louder than words, and people set
their course accordingly. For example, two days after Diem's
assassination, Prince Sihanouk of Cambodia said he no longer
would accept American aid. If that was how the United States
treated its friends, he did not care to be a friend.

The Vietnam War proved that the United States, despite its
large military armed with sophisticated weaponry, was not om-
nipotent. Some have acted on that realization. Take, for instance, the Ayatollah Khomeini. In 1979, his fanatical Iranian
followers took over the American embassy in Tehran and held
fifty-three American embassy employees hostage for more than
a year. American diplomatic efforts to gain their immediate
release were a failure. An American military effort to rescue the
hostages also was a failure. The United States had lost its aura of
moral righteousness and military invincibility.

A revolutionary guard on the wall of the U.S. Embassy in Tehran—his feet resting on photographs of American troops in Vietnam—shortly after the taking of the American hostages

20
Sorting It Out

When the United States finally withdrew from the Vietnam War, most Americans wished to relegate the entire business to the past. Both those who saw it as a noble cause and those who saw it as a wrong cause hoped that Vietnam, like a bad dream, could soon be forgotten.

Nonetheless, many Americans grudgingly agreed with a few Vietnam veterans that there should be a memorial in honor of all those who lost their lives or were listed as missing during the war. A competition for designs was announced.

The winning design was submitted by Maya Yang Lin, then a student in architecture at Yale University. Her architectural renderings showed two polished granite slabs set at an angle into a soft bank of land in Washington, D.C. The massive tablets bear the names of the 57,939 Americans who died in Vietnam or are listed as missing in action.

The war memorial's abstract design is powerfully elegant. It is also powerfully quiet. It moves people who hold vastly different opinions about the war. For some, the memorial summons a sense of sober dignity. For others, it is a stark testimony to the sheer waste of the war. Reading the names of the Vietnam

War's dead and missing, viewers also see their own image reflected in the polished stone. Like the Vietnam War itself, the memorial speaks of Americans who died and of Americans who are living; of Vietnam and of the United States; of the past and of the present—and, by implication, of the future.

The dedication of the Vietnam War Memorial, on November 13, 1982, gave long overdue recognition to American soldiers for the efforts and sacrifices they made in their nation's behalf. It also signaled Americans' willingness to come to terms with what the war meant and means for us. The freshening debate of the last few years is entirely healthy. Just as we are meant to see ourselves today in the Vietnam War Memorial's reflection, it is important that we see ourselves in our thinking about the Vietnam War. The war raised so many questions about us. Until we answer those questions, our image—as individuals and as a nation—will be as transparent and insubstantial as a reflection in polished granite.

To begin, to what extent does communism threaten us? In the late 1960s, American foreign policy–makers began exploring ways to foster peaceful coexistence with Communist countries. Can we indeed get along with Communist countries, or is the pursuit of peaceful coexistence merely a way of making the best of a bad situation?

If communism threatens our security, how are we going to fight it? Are we going to go to battle, as we did in Vietnam, when communism makes its bid for power? Some doves, like the professor of religion Robert McAfee Brown, believe that such wars are not the proper way to contain communism:

> Communism is an attempt (tragically wrong, we believe) to combat poverty. As long as we fight Communism, poverty will increase. If we fight poverty (which Communism feeds on), Communism will lose its appeal.[20]

Perhaps Vietnam was lost to communism because the fight against communism was begun too late. If Brown is right—if we can fight communism only by fighting poverty—we will need to replace military tactics with economic tactics.

If the United States cannot be policeman for the whole world, which countries will we assist and which will we not assist? Should we have continued to help the South Vietnamese when their various regimes proved uninterested in democratic systems? Should we have continued to send in our combat troops when many South Vietnamese military leaders proved unwilling to lead the fight for their own country, their own freedom?

In deciding on which countries we will assist, does geography play a role? Is a Communist Nicaragua more threatening than a Communist Vietnam, or has technology shrunk the world so much that both are of equal concern?

What conditions will we set when we offer aid to another country? Some believe that the United States had a right to require certain programs in South Vietnam on the basis of our massive amount of aid. But others believe that such requirements are a high-handed expression of American "superiority." Our way is not necessarily the only way. In addition, our way, often going against the values of another people, can be self-defeating. Unaware of what home means to the Vietnamese, Americans promoted pacification programs that created a sea of refugees and alienated the very people we were trying to assist.

Have we the emotional stamina to sustain an active American role in shaping the world order? Looking back on the Vietnam War, Henry Kissinger observed, "For a great power to abandon a small country to tyranny simply to obtain a respite from our own travail seemed to me—and still seems to me—profoundly immoral and destructive of our efforts to build a new and ultimately more peaceful pattern of international relations."[21]

What are we willing to give up in programs at home to fight communism abroad or even just to maintain a huge military at the ready? The Vietnam War proved beyond doubt that Amer-

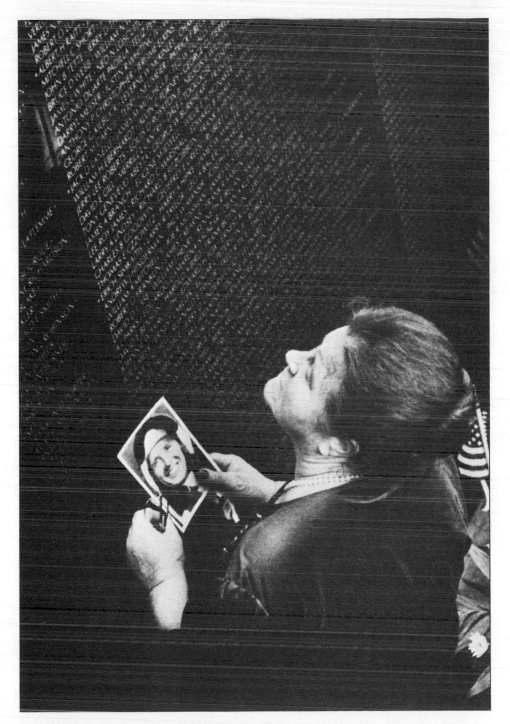

A mother hunting for her son's name on the Vietnam War Memorial

icans cannot have everything. Although the United States is the richest country in the world, great numbers of our own citizens live in poverty. Imagine the food, job training, and housing that the $165 billion we spent on the war could have bought for our needy at home.

What kind of weaponry are we willing to use in military conflicts? Although we did not use the nuclear weapons in the American arsenal, many in both the U.S. military and the public at large felt we lost the war because we didn't use all that was available to us. Others disagree, saying that some tools of war gain us only hollow victories; napalm, Agent Orange, nuclear weapons—all take a grotesque toll, often with costs that show up only many years later. Is a victory earned with such weapons worth the cost to our fellow human beings?

Whom will we send to fight? There is no doubt that the draft system was unfair in its treatment of the Vietnam War generation. We need to decide which deferments and exemptions are proper. Further, we need to decide what we expect of women in terms of national service.

The rights of free speech and dissent are fundamental to all that the United States stands for. Or so we say. During the Vietnam War, many Americans were saddened by what the antiwar movement provoked. They were appalled to see students attacking National Guard centers on American campuses. They were appalled to see Chicago police clubbing chanting protesters outside the 1968 Democratic national convention. What are the appropriate ways to express and respond to dissent? Was black activist Stokely Carmichael's hope for Ho Chi Minh's victory a responsible political stance? What about the hardhats' motto, "My country, love it or leave it"?

These are but a few of the questions raised by the Vietnam War. All concern what the United States means to us. All concern what we think the United States is and what it can become. All concern patriotism in the very best sense of the word.

Afterword

For Americans, Vietnam is now far more than just a country on a map. The very name Vietnam brings to mind a welter of images. We see the lovely Vietnamese woman in her *ao dai*; we see the Buddhist monk in his saffron robe, aflame. We see Vietnamese peasants uprooted from their own and their ancestors' homes; we see the body bags of American dead waiting to be shipped home. We see a South Vietnamese president assassinated by his own armed forces; we see an American president unable to run as his own party's nominee. We see a helicopter crash and burn; we see Americans tear up and burn draft cards. We see our shimmering selves in the Vietnam War Memorial.

So varied and confused are all these images that we hardly know where to begin to put them all together to form one big picture. So saddening, even horrifying, are all these images that we hardly *want* to put them all together to form one big picture.

In fact, we long to forget Vietnam. In trying to erase those images that Vietnam brings to mind, we try to erase all those questions that Vietnam raises. With time, the images will grow dimmer. But the questions will grow more pressing. Until we answer those questions, the United States—as a people and as a nation—will be out of focus and out of joint. Until we decide what we stand for, what we will fight for, and how we will fight for it, we will be unable to propose a meaningful national policy. Without a meaningful national policy, we will find ourselves defeated, not just in Vietnam, but at home too.

Glossary

Accord: the diplomatic term for an agreement.

Agent Orange: a chemical defoliant that can cause cancer.

Annam: the thin central area of Vietnam connecting the north, often called Tonkin, and the south, often called Cochinchina.

ARVN: the acronym, pronounced Ar-vin, for the Army of the Republic of (South) Vietnam.

Atrocity: an unusual act of brutality totally outside accepted standards of behavior.

Bonze: a Buddhist monk.

Buddhism: a religion originating in India that addresses suffering.

Carcinogen: a cancer-causing agent.

Cell: the smallest unit of people in the Communist organizational system.

Cochinchina: the southern area of Vietnam, dominated by the Mekong River delta.

Cold War: rivalry between hostile nations up to but not including military conflict.

Colony: a geographical area separate from but ruled by another nation.

GLOSSARY

Communism: the system of social groupings in which all members share ownership of property.

Confucianism: the moral system developed in China by which the individual seeks harmony with his world by subordinating his or her needs and desires to those of the family, community, and state.

Conscientious objection: the refusal to enter the military on the grounds that all war is wrong.

Counterinsurgency: a program for fighting guerrilla war.

Coup d'état: the overthrow of a government by violence.

Court-martial: a military trial.

Credibility gap: the distrust arising from the discrepancy between what is done and what is said to be done.

Defoliant: a herbicide used to kill vegetation.

Domino theory: the belief that when one country falls under Communist domination, its neighbors will soon fall to the same fate.

Dove: one who advocated a U.S. withdrawal from the Vietnam War.

Draft: the system of selecting men for the armed services.

Draft dodger: one who avoids the draft.

Dynasty: a succession of rulers from one family line.

Fragging: the wounding or killing of officers by their own men, using weapons such as fragmentation grenades.

Guerrilla: a member of a small fighting force that harasses an enemy in ambushes.

Guerrilla war: a war in which a small, poorly armed force fights— usually by means of ambush—a large, well-armed force.

Hawk: one who advocated the U.S. military effort in Vietnam.

Ho Chi Minh Trail: jungle paths cut through southern Laos and northeastern Cambodia to the highlands of South Vietnam.

Immolate: to set fire to.

Indochina: the Asian land mass comprising Vietnam, Laos, and Cambodia.

Junta: a small group acting as an interim government, particularly after a coup d'état.

MACV: the acronym, pronounced Mac-vee, for (U.S.) Military Assistance Command, Vietnam.

Mandarin: a scholar in the emperor's court who served as a government bureaucrat.

Matériel: military supplies.

Napalm: a jellylike substance, used in weapons, that causes prolonged burning.

Nationalist: one who favors independence for his or her country.

National Liberation Front (NLF): the organization of insurgents formed in South Vietnam in 1960.

New Economic Area (NEA): an agricultural area cleared by the Communist regime to accommodate refugees within Vietnam and to increase food production.

Oligarchy: a small, closely knit governing group.

Pacification: the program to protect and win the support of people living in rural areas.

Parallel hierarchy: a complete local government existing side by side with its formally recognized counterpart.

Partition: the division of a country into separately governed parts.

Protectorate: a small state protected and partly controlled by a larger state.

Post-Vietnam Syndrome (PVS): the emotional stress American combat troops experienced as a result of the Vietnam War.

Puppet: a titular head of government whose decisions and actions are determined by an outside power.

Quoc Ngu: the romanized writing system developed for the Vietnamese language by Alexandre de Rhodes.

Republic: an independent state governed by its own citizens.

Sanctuary: a safe place for guerrillas to prepare for fighting or to regroup after fighting.

Self-criticism: a Communist technique of discussing one's own and others' errors to refine tactics and bond individuals to a group.

Sino-Soviet split: the tension between China and the USSR, dating from the late 1950s.

Tet: the Confucian holiday during the lunar new year when the Spirit of the Hearth is believed to retire to the Palace of Jade in heaven and Confucianists pay respect to their departed ancestors.

Tonkin: the northern area of Vietnam, dominated by the Red River delta.

Vietcong: the nickname, meaning "Vietnamese Communist," first applied by the Diem regime, for members of the NLF.

Vietminh: the nickname for members of the Vietnam Doc Lap Dong Minh, the nationalist—and Communist—organization established by Ho Chi Minh in 1941.

Vietnamization: the process by which the ARVN was to take over the war in Vietnam.

Notes

PART I. The Field of Battle

1. The complete text of Ho's Declaration of Independence of the Democratic Republic of Vietnam appears in *Vietnam: Anthology and Guide to A Television History*, edited by Steven Cohen (New York: Alfred A. Knopf, 1983), pp. 24–26.
2. The legend of Lac Long Quan and Au Co and the Hong Bang dynasty is drawn from Walter J. Sheldon's *Tigers in the Rice: The Story of Vietnam from Ancient Past to Uncertain Future* (London: Crowell-Collier Press, 1969), pp. 2–3.
3. Statistics on Vietnamese schools and literacy are quoted in Dean Brelis and Jill Krementz's *The Face of South Vietnam* (Boston: Houghton Mifflin Company, 1968), p. 4.
4. Leclerc's analysis of what French troop needs would be is quoted in David Halberstam's *Ho* (New York: Random House, 1971), p. 84.
5. The United States's contribution to France's war effort appears in *The Pentagon Papers*, as published by *The New York Times* (New York: Bantam Books, 1971), p. 10.

PART II. Americans Take to the Field of Battle

1. David Halberstam, *The Making of a Quagmire* (New York: Random House, 1965), p. 52.
2. The United States's view of the 1954 Geneva agreement is reprinted in *The Pentagon Papers*, as published by *The New York Times*, p. 1.
3. Statistics for the movement of Vietnamese between the North and the South vary. The numbers for Vietminh troops and their sympathizers who moved to the North appear in Robert Shaplen's *The Lost Revolution: The Story of Twenty Years of Neglected Opportunities in Vietnam and America's Failure to Foster Democracy There* (New York: Harper & Row, 1965), p. 114. Statistics on the civilian emigration from the North to the South are provided by Bernard Fall in *The Two Viet-Nams: A Political and Military Analysis*, 2d rev. ed. (New York: Frederick A. Praeger, 1967), pp. 152–53.
4. Fall's suggestion concerning the North's willingness to allow temporary food shortages is discussed in *The Two Viet-Nams*, p. 160.
5. Eisenhower's appraisal of Diem's chances in national elections is recounted in Michael Novak's essay "Stumbling into War and Stumbling Out," in *Vietnam: Crisis of Conscience*, by Robert McAfee Brown, Abraham J. Heschel, and Michael Novak (New York: Association Press, Herder and Herder, and Behrman House, 1967), p. 25.
6. The assessment of the damage to the old Vietminh cell structure is provided by Stanley Karnow in *Vietnam: A History* (New York: Viking Press, 1983), p. 227.
7. The Vietcong's knowledge of political theory is discussed by Frances FitzGerald in *Fire in the Lake: The Vietnamese and the Americans in Vietnam* (Boston: Atlantic Monthly Press/Little, Brown and Company, 1972), p. 218.
8. The extent of the NLF presence in 1962 is drawn from FitzGerald's *Fire in the Lake*, p. 149.
9. Kennedy's comment to Reston appears in Karnow's *Vietnam: A History*, p. 248.

10. Madame Nhu's view of Buddhist immolations and an explanation for her use of the word "barbecue" are discussed by Marguerite Higgins in *Our Vietnam Nightmare* (New York: Harper & Row, 1965), pp. 71–73.

11. Kennedy's question to Krulak and Mendenhall is quoted in Higgins's *Our Vietnam Nightmare*, p. 104.

PART III. The American War in Vietnam

1. Michael Herr, *Dispatches* (New York: Alfred A. Knopf, 1977), p. 71.

2. Johnson's reassurance that the United States would keep its commitments, delivered in a speech to a joint session of Congress, appears in his memoirs, *The Vantage Point: Perspectives of the Presidency, 1963–1969* (New York: Holt, Rinehart and Winston, 1971), p. xi.

3. De Gaulle's warning to Kennedy is quoted in Karnow's *Vietnam: A History*, p. 248.

4. Kennedy's remark to Mansfield about an American withdrawal from Vietnam is quoted in Barbara W. Tuchman's *The March of Folly: From Troy to Vietnam* (New York: Alfred A. Knopf, 1984), p. 303.

5. Lodge's cable is quoted in Karnow's *Vietnam: A History*, p. 311.

6. Herrick's review of the "second attack" on the *Maddox* appears in Sheldon's *Tigers in the Rice*, p. 98.

7. Johnson's opinion on what might have attacked the *Maddox* on the second day in the Gulf of Tonkin is quoted in David Halberstam's *The Best and the Brightest* (New York: Random House, 1972), p. 414.

8. What Johnson told Ky he wanted appears in Richard Critchfield's *The Long Charade: Political Subversion in the Vietnam War* (New York: Harcourt Brace Jovanovich, 1968), p. 216.

9. Johnson's view of how he would have fared in the 1968 election and of his ability to retain the public's support appears in *The Vantage Point*, pp. 549, 550.

10. Nixon's comment on when the Vietnam War would become his war appears in Tuchman's *The March of Folly*, p. 358.
11. Nixon's view of what successful negotiation requires is quoted from his *RN: The Memoirs of Richard Nixon* (New York: Grosset & Dunlap, 1978), p. 269.
12. Karnow offers estimates of Communist casualty figures during the 1972 offensive in *Vietnam: A History*, p. 643.
13. The tonnage of bombs dropped on North Vietnam during Linebacker Two is drawn from Karnow's *Vietnam: A History*, p. 653.

PART IV. The Vietnam War in America

1. Gloria Emerson, *Winners and Losers: Battles, Retreats, Gains, Losses and Ruins from a Long War* (New York: Random House, 1976), p. 37.
2. Eisenhower's simile that gave rise to the term *domino theory* appears in Fall's *The Two Viet-Nams*, p. 225.
3. Higgins's view of Vietnam as a front line of freedom is taken from *Our Vietnam Nightmare*, p. ix.
4. The remark about Diem as a willful puppet appears in Karnow's *Vietnam: A History*, p. 235.
5. Kennan's assessment of Communist unity is outlined by Novak in *Vietnam: Crisis of Conscience*, p. 16.
6. Fall's suggestion that American concern about China would make support for the North logical appears in *The Two Viet-Nams*, p. 407.
7. Kennan's view that communism is changing is drawn from Novak's essay in *Vietnam: Crisis of Conscience*, p. 16.
8. The oft-quoted statement of why Bentre was destroyed appears in Karnow's *Vietnam: A History*, p. 534.
9. Bundy's view of what a communiqué should say is quoted in Phillip Knightley's *The First Casualty, from the Crimea to Vietnam: The War Correspondent as Hero, Propagandist, and Myth Maker* (New York: Harvest/Harcourt Brace Jovanovich, 1976), p. 380.

10. Halberstam's view of how *Time* magazine editors view the magazine is from his *The Making of a Quagmire*, p. 269.

11. The problems the press encountered during the early years in Vietnam are based on an account by Knightley in *The First Casualty*, pp. 374–81.

12. Knightley's view that the press addressed only one of two problems in Vietnam is presented in *The First Casualty*, p. 380.

13. The Johnson administration's problem with Salisbury's report of civilian bombing in the North is outlined by Mary McCarthy in *Vietnam* (New York: Harcourt Brace Jovanovich, 1967), p. 99.

14. The Pentagon's nickname for Salisbury appears in Knightley's *The First Casualty*, p. 416.

15. Arlen's point that television diminished the reality of the Vietnam War is quoted from his essay "Living-Room War," which appears in a collection of essays under the same title (New York: Viking Press, 1969), p. 8.

16. Herr's term *movie-fed war fantasies* is quoted from his *Dispatches*, p. 194.

17. The marine officer's outburst is drawn from Knightley's *The First Casualty*, p. 405.

18. Karnow's view that the press followed public opinion appears in his *Vietnam: A History*, p. 488.

19. Fallows's summary of Ferber's point is to be found in *The Wounded Generation: America After Vietnam*, edited by A. D. Horne (Englewood Cliffs, N.J.: A Washington Post Book, Prentice-Hall, 1981), p. 21.

20. A complete breakdown of the Vietnam generation and the draft is provided in a chart in *The Wounded Generation*, p. 6.

21. Fallows's view on the connection between who fought the war and the length of the war is drawn from *The Wounded Generation*, pp. 20, 103.

22. Tuchman's appraisal of how protest affected the general public appears in *The March of Folly*, pp. 339, 327.

23. Mitchell's comparison of the second Vietnam Moratorium Day with the Russian Revolution is quoted in Tuchman's *The March of Folly*, p. 362.

PART V. After the Battle

1. Norman Podhoretz, *Why We Were in Vietnam* (New York: Simon and Schuster, 1982), p. 197.
2. Karnow's evaluation of the strength of the Thieu regime at the time the Paris peace accords were signed appears in his *Vietnam: A History*, p. 657.
3. Kissinger's analysis of who wins in a guerrilla war is to be found in his memoirs *White House Years* (Boston: Little, Brown and Company, 1979), p. 232.
4. The extent of collectivization in the Mekong delta is quoted from Craig R. Whitney's "A Bitter Peace," *The New York Times Magazine*, October 30, 1983, p. 58.
5. Whitney's figure for the number of people fleeing Vietnam, which covers the period 1975–1983, appears in "A Bitter Peace," p. 60.
6. Pham Van Dong's lament about the difficulty of governing is quoted by Karnow in *Vietnam: A History*, p. 9.
7. Harris poll statistics on the public's attitude toward Vietnam veterans appears in *The Wounded Generation*, p. 90.
8. The man who was so ashamed by our defeat is quoted by Emerson in *Winners and Losers*, p. 295.
9. Page's belief that war is glamorous is quoted by Knightley in *The First Casualty*, p. 407.
10. Knightley's opinion that Mylai is not an atrocity is quoted from *The First Casualty*, p. 393.
11. Drug use among American soldiers in Vietnam is discussed by Karnow in *Vietnam: A History*, p. 23.
12. The average ages of soldiers in World War II and the Vietnam War are provided by Karnow in *Vietnam: A History*, p. 26.
13. Dean Phillips recounts his experience with a law-school admissions committee in *The Wounded Generation*, pp. 114–15.
14. Damage to the military is discussed by Halberstam in *The Best and the Brightest*, p. 657.
15. The cost of the Vietnam War is quoted from *The Wounded Generation*, p. 5.
16. Figures for the cost of the war in fiscal year 1968 and the deficit

for that same year are provided by Halberstam in *The Best and the Brightest*, pp. 608–9.

17. The figure for the projected budget deficit for fiscal-year 1986 appears in *The New York Times*, November 15, 1984, p. 1.

18. McNaughton's summary of U.S. aims in Vietnam appears in *The Pentagon Papers*, p. 432.

19. Samuel Brown's concern about the need to restore trust is quoted from *The Wounded Generation*, p. 189.

20. Robert McAfee Brown's view of the appropriate way to fight communism appears in his essay "An Appeal to the Churches and Synagogues," in *Vietnam: Crisis of Conscience*, p. 81.

21. Kissinger's view of the implications of our abandonment of South Vietnam appears in his *White House Years*, p. 228.

Bibliography

Many good books on Vietnam have already been published, and many more are sure to follow. Nonetheless, it is hard to imagine a general history surpassing Stanley Karnow's *Vietnam: A History* (New York: Viking Press, 1983). Comprehensive, eminently readable, it is essential reading for anyone interested in the Vietnam War.

Karnow's book is the companion volume to "Vietnam: A Television History," PBS's thirteen-part series for which Karnow served as chief correspondent. Yet another book published in connection with the television series is *Vietnam: Anthology and Guide to A Television History*, edited by Steven Cohen (New York: Alfred A. Knopf, 1983). Following the organization of the PBS series, this book is particularly useful for its short historical summaries, chronologies, and a diverse selection of documents ranging from government analyses to antiwar folk songs.

Another particularly good overview is *The Eyewitness History of the Vietnam War: 1961–1975* by George Esper and The Associated Press (New York: Ballantine Books, 1983), which is lavishly illustrated.

An especially valuable book is Frances FitzGerald's *Fire in the Lake: The Vietnamese and the Americans in Vietnam* (Boston: Atlantic Monthly Press/Little, Brown and Company, 1972). Here one will find an exploration of how American policies conflicted with age-old Vietnamese values and outlooks.

Ngo Dinh Diem has been extensively considered in a variety of books about the Vietnam War. Ho Chi Minh, on the other hand, is more of a mystery, which he himself did much to foster. A good biography is David Halberstam's *Ho* (New York: Random House, 1971).

An exciting book that chronicles the end of the French control of Vietnam and describes the determination and tactics of the Vietminh is Jules Roy's *The Battle of Dienbienphu*, translated from the French by Robert Baldick (New York: Harper & Row, 1965).

A number of excellent histories were published while the United States was still engaged in the war. A particularly eminent book is Bernard Fall's *The Two Viet-Nams: A Political and Military Analysis*, second revised edition (New York: Frederick A. Praeger, 1967). Other recommended books are *Tigers in the Rice: The Story of Vietnam from Ancient Past to Uncertain Future* by Walter J. Sheldon (London: Crowell-Collier Press, 1969); *The Lost Revolution: The Story of Twenty Years of Neglected Opportunities in Vietnam and of America's Failure to Foster Democracy There* by Robert Shaplen (New York: Harper & Row, 1965); and *A Short Introduction to the History and Politics of Southeast Asia* by Richard A. Allen (New York: Oxford University Press, 1970). This last is of special interest because Vietnam is seen in a larger geographical context.

Marguerite Higgins, one of the few journalists who staunchly supported the Diem regime in both its goals and approaches, is the author of *Our Vietnam Nightmare* (New York: Harper & Row, 1965). This book gives extensive coverage to the Ngos and the Buddhist crisis. Richard Critchfield, who covered South Vietnam from 1964 to 1967, offers a good look at events during that period in *The Long Charade: Political Subversion in the Vietnam War* (New York: Harcourt Brace Jovanovich, 1968). *The Face of South Vietnam* (Boston: Houghton Mifflin Company, 1968), comprising an essay by Dean Brelis and photographs by Jill Krementz, gives a particularly good sense of what South Vietnam was like during the war.

A slim book that provides a powerful description of pacification is

Jonathan Schell's *The Village of Ben Suc* (New York: Alfred A. Knopf, 1967). For an idea of what combat is like, Ronald Glasser's *365 Days* (New York: George Braziller, 1980) is recommended. "Cincinnatus" is the pen name for Cecil B. Currey, who as a member of the Pentagon staff wrote *Self-Destruction: The Disintegration and Decay of the United States Army During the Vietnam Era* (New York: W. W. Norton, 1981), a scathing indictment of the prosecution of the Vietnam War.

The art and history of war reportage can be found in Phillip Knightley's *The First Casualty, from the Crimea to Vietnam: The War Correspondent as Hero, Propagandist, and Myth Maker* (New York: Harvest/Harcourt Brace Jovanovich, 1976). David Halberstam's *The Making of a Quagmire* (New York: Random House, 1965) gives a good idea of how correspondents work, as well as a view of the guerrilla war in the early 1960s. Michael Herr's *Dispatches* (New York: Alfred A. Knopf, 1977) is a vivid account of a correspondent working at the height of the war. Michael J. Arlen offers a number of thoughtful essays on television and the Vietnam War in *Living-Room War* (New York: Viking Press, 1969).

An interesting philosophical analysis of the draft, prepared by the American Friends Service Committee, is *The Draft?* (New York: Hill and Wang, 1968).

Among the intellectuals who used their pens in opposition to the war is Mary McCarthy, author of *Vietnam* (New York: Harcourt Brace Jovanovich, 1967) and *Hanoi* (New York: Harcourt Brace Jovanovich, 1968). Members of the religious community also wrote in opposition to the war. One book with a religious orientation is *Vietnam: Crisis of Conscience* by Robert McAfee Brown, Abraham J. Heschel, and Michael Novak (New York: Association Press, Herder and Herder, and Behrman House, 1967).

David Halberstam's *The Best and the Brightest* (New York: Random House, 1972) is a fascinating book that describes who made American policy in Vietnam and why.

The approximately four thousand pages of documents and three thousand pages of narrative history that make up the study of Vietnam commissioned in 1967 by Robert McNamara were edited and appear in text form in *The Pentagon Papers* as published by *The New York Times* (New York: Bantam Books, 1971). This provides an unusual look at how policy was made.

The memoirs of decision-makers also are of interest, although their value is diminished by the formality of the genre. The reader is referred to Lyndon Baines Johnson's *The Vantage Point: Perspectives of the Presidency, 1963–1969* (New York: Holt, Rinehart and Winston, 1971); Richard Nixon's *RN: The Memoirs of Richard Nixon* (New York: Grosset & Dunlap, 1978); and Henry Kissinger's *White House Years* (Boston: Little, Brown and Company, 1979). All three have organized their books so that Vietnam is treated in separate chapters.

William J. Duiker offers a comprehensive view of Vietnam since 1975 in *Vietnam Since the Fall of Saigon*, Papers in International Studies, Southeast Asia Series no. 56 (Athens, Ohio: Ohio University Press, 1980). There are also a number of books about the United States since the American withdrawal. Especially valuable are *The Wounded Generation: America After Vietnam*, edited by A. D. Horne (Englewood Cliffs, N.J.: A Washington Post Book, Prentice-Hall, 1981), and Gloria Emerson's *Winners and Losers: Battles, Retreats, Gains, Losses and Ruins from a Long War* (New York: Random House, 1976).

A thoughtful analysis of what atrocities like the Mylai massacre represent can be found in Mary McCarthy's *Medina* (New York: Harcourt Brace Jovanovich, 1972).

As Americans gain more perspective, more will be written about whether the Vietnam War should have been waged. Two books in that area are recommended: Norman Podhoretz's *Why We Were in Vietnam* (New York: Simon and Schuster, 1982) and Barbara W. Tuchman's *The March of Folly: From Troy to Vietnam* (New York: Alfred A. Knopf, 1984).

Acknowledgments

It seems somewhat misleading that an author's name should enjoy such solitary prominence on a book's jacket, spine, and title page. Most books come into being only because of an author's many silent partners—at least, that has been my experience. The first silent partner I should like to thank is Jonathan Lanman, my editor, who proposed this project to me. At every step of the way, he has proved a marvelous, sensitive sounding board.

My father, Vincent Jones, has always been interested in Asia, but especially so since 1967, when he visited Southeast Asia, including South Vietnam, as a journalist. He was most helpful in getting me launched, providing me with books he had found particularly useful, as well as with his own perceptive essays written in connection with that trip and suggestions for the photographs.

Being a research project, this book is based on the work of many observant, eloquent writers. Two very kindly helped me with questions that persisted: George Esper of the Associated Press and Stanley Karnow. I am also indebted to Tran Trong Kahnn, of the Permanent Mission of the Socialist Republic of Vietnam to the United Nations, for vetting the pronunciations and helping with the map. Any errors that remain are, of course, my responsibility.

ACKNOWLEDGMENTS

Anne Zaroff read with her remarkably keen intelligence an early draft of the manuscript and gently pointed out grotesqueries, from dangling participles to foggy thought.

Photographs could not have been gathered with such ease and pleasure without the efficiency and graciousness of Frank Hyatt and Walter Mosby of Wide World Photos.

My essential silent partner is my husband, James Mabie. A genie with a word processor, he magically produced one after another pristine draft. All the while, he stoically tolerated more haphazard dinners than the law would allow. A good man may be hard to find, but I did it.

Index

Agent Orange, 126
Apbac, battle at, 50–51
Arlen, Michael, 108–9
ARVN (Army of the Republic of Vietnam), 48–51, 53, 54, 70, 72, 75–76, 78, 84–85, 86, 87, 98, 103
  after U.S. withdrawal, 119, 120, 121
  coup against Diem and, 52, 54, 56–57
  Vietnamization of the war, 76–77, 78–80, 83
Associated Press, 53
Atrocities of the Vietnam War, 126–28
Au Co, 4

Bao Dai, 22, 23, 25, 33, 34, 36, 39, 43

Bay of Pigs invasion, 46
Bigart, Homer, 103, 104
Binh Xuyen, 39
Boat people, Vietnamese, 122–24
Brown, Robert McAfee, 137
Brown, Samuel, 114, 134
Browne, Malcolm, 53
Buddhism and Buddhists, 6, 11, 52–54, 141
Bundy, McGeorge, 104

C. Turner Joy, 64
Calley, William, 128
Cambodia, 33, 77–78, 80, 81, 84, 100, 108, 119, 124, 132, 133, 134
Carlton Hotel, London, 20
Carmichael, Stokely, 140
Carter, Jimmy, 124

Castro, Fidel, 46
Catholic missionaries, 10–15
Chiang Kai-shek, 21, 26
Children fathered by American soldiers in Vietnam, 128–29
China, 15–16, 20–21, 24
  Communist, see People's Republic of China
  Vietnam ruled by, 4–8
Clifford, Clark, 72, 73
Cochinchina, 15, 16, 24, 25
Communism, 91–96, 99–100, 102, 137–38
Confucianism, 11
Conscientious objection, 111
Cuba, 46

Dai Viet, 22
D'Argenlieu, Georges Thierry, 25
De Gaulle, Charles, 62
Defoliants, 126
Democratic Republic of Vietnam, see North Vietnam
Dienbienphu, 29–30, 33, 95
Domino theory, 93–94
Doves, 97–102, 115
Draft, the, 111–14, 131, 140, 141
Drug use, 129
Dupré, Jules-Marie, 15
Dupuis, Jean, 15

Eastern Europe, 28, 93, 94
Eisenhower, Dwight D., 30, 43, 46, 94
Ellsberg, Daniel, 133
Escoffier, Georges Auguste, 20

Fall, Bernard, 38, 100
Fallows, James, 112
Ferber, Michael, 112
FitzGerald, Frances, 45
Fourteen Points, 20
France, 9, 20, 23, 24, 36, 62, 97
  during World War II, 21, 22
  gains control of Vietnam, 14, 15–18
  Geneva Conference and, 33, 34
  Indochina War, 24–30, 33, 38, 94, 98
Future foreign policy of the United States, 140–42

Geneva accords, 33–37, 43, 44, 49, 98
Geneva Conference of 1954, 28, 30, 33–37, 82
Germany, 20, 21, 67
GI Bill of Rights, 130
Gia Long, see Nguyen Anh
Goldwater, Barry, 65
Gracey, Douglas, 24
Great Britain, 24, 33
Guerrilla warfare, 6, 26, 120
Gulf of Tonkin Resolution, 64, 65, 132

Halberstam, David, 105–6, 131
Harkins, Paul D., 50
Harriman, W. Averell, 74
Harvard University, 112
Hawks, 91–96, 100
Herr, Michael, 109
Herrick, John, 64
Hersh, Seymour, 128

Higgins, Marguerite, 95
History of Vietnam, 4–23
  before Western influence, 4–9
  French gain control, 14–18
  Indochina War, 24–30, 38, 94, 98
  rise of the nationalists, 18–23, 97
  Vietnam War, *see* North Vietnam; South Vietnam; United States
  Western missionaries, 10–15
Ho Chi Minh, 18, 20, 23, 36, 43, 80, 97, 140
  before organizing the Vietminh, 18–21
  declares Vietnam's independence, 22
  Indochina War and, 24–30
  rules North Vietnam, 38–39
  Vietminh during World War II and, 21–22
Ho Chi Minh Trail, 83
Hong, 4
Hong Bang dynasty, Vietnam, 4
Humphrey, Hubert, 74

Indochina War, 24–30, 38, 94, 98
Industrial Revolution, 91
Iran hostage crisis, 135
Israel, 99

Japan, 21–22, 23, 24, 97, 99
Johnson, Lyndon Baines, and Johnson administration, 61–74, 81, 106–8, 132, 133, 134

Kennan, George, 99–100
Kennedy, John F., and Kennedy administration, 36, 46, 49, 54–56, 57, 61, 104, 106, 132, 134
Kennedy, Robert, 133
Kent State University, 80
Khomeini, Ayatollah, 134
Khrushchev, Nikita, 46
Kissinger, Henry, 77, 78, 81–82, 86, 87–88, 120, 138
Knightley, Phillip, 106, 108, 128
Korean War, 28, 30, 33, 66, 94
Krulak, Victor, 56

Lac Long Quan, 4
Lamson 719, 84–85
Lansdale, Edward, 37, 39–40, 52
Laos, 33, 81, 84, 101
Le Duc Tho, 81–82, 86, 87–88
Le Loi, 7–8, 25
Lefèvre, Dominique, 14
Lenin, Nikolai, 20
Lin, Maya Yang, 136
Lodge, Henry Cabot, 54, 62
Lon Nol, 80
Louis XVI, King of France, 12

McCarthy, Eugene, 133
McNamara, Robert, 70–72, 73
McNaughton, John, 132–133
Maddox, 64, 65
Mansfield, Mike, 36, 62
Mao Zedong, 26–27, 45–46, 94
Martin, Graham, 122

Marx, Karl, 91–92
Maryknoll Institute, 36
Mecklin, John, 105
Media coverage of Vietnam War, 103–9
Medina, Ernest, 128
Mendenhall, Joseph A., 56
Military Assistance Command, Vietnam (MACV), 50, 51
Minh Mang, 12
Missionaries, 10–15
Mitchell, John, 115
Mohr, Charles, 105
Mylai massacre, 126–28

National Liberation Front (NLF) (Vietcong), 45–46, 48–49, 50–51, 65, 70–73, 75–76, 78–80, 86, 87
    see also North Vietnam
Nationalists, rise of Vietnamese, 18–23, 97
    see also Vietminh organization
New Economic Areas (NEAs), 123
New York Times, The, 48, 79, 85–86, 103, 105–6, 128
New Yorker, The, 108
Ngo Dinh Diem, 23, 36, 37, 39, 40–43, 44, 98, 99, 103–4
    the coup overthrowing, 52–57, 62, 82, 134, 141
Ngo Dinh Khoi, 23
Ngo Dinh Nhu, 39, 40, 54, 56–57
Ngo Dinh Thuc, 40
Nguyen Ai Quoc, 20

Nguyen Anh (Gia Long), 12, 14
Nguyen Cao Ky, 71
Nguyen family, 8, 9, 12, 34
Nguyen Sinh Cung, see Ho Chi Minh
Nguyen Sinh Sac, 18
Nguyen Van Thieu, 75, 76, 77, 82, 87, 88, 119, 120, 122
Nhu, Madame, 40, 54
Nixon, Richard, and Nixon administration, 74–87, 100, 115, 119, 124, 125, 130, 132, 133–34
Nolting, Frederick, 54
North Vietnam, 37, 38–39, 43, 65, 75–76, 80, 98–102
    after U.S. withdrawal, 119–23
    beginning of insurgency against the South, 44–51
    bombing of, 65, 66–67, 68, 70–71, 74, 81, 87, 99, 102, 106–8, 132
    creation of, 34
    media coverage of the war, 103–9
    National Liberation Front, see National Liberation Front
    peace negotiations and agreement with, 76, 77, 81–88, 108, 119
    Tet Offensive and, 72–73, 78
    Vietcong, see National Liberation Front
    see also South Vietnam; Vietnam
Nuclear weapons, 115

Operation Rolling Thunder, *see* North Vietnam, bombing of

Page, Tim, 126
Paris, France, 20
  peace negotiations and agreement, 76, 77, 81–88, 108, 119, 120, 125
Pentagon papers, 85–86, 134
People's Republic of China, 26–28, 33–34, 67, 94, 101, 124
  see also China
Pham Van Dong, 124
Phillips, Dean, 130
Phoenix program, 78
Phu Quoc (island), 12
Pigneau de Béhaine, Pierre Joseph Georges, 12
Piroth, Charles, 30
Portugal, 10, 11
Post-Vietnam Syndrome (PVS), 129–30
Poulo Condore Island, 14
Psychological problems of Vietnam veterans, 129–30

Quang Duc, Thich, 53
Quoc Ngu (writing system), 10, 18

Refugees from Vietnam, 122–24
Republic of Vietnam, *see* South Vietnam
Reston, James, 46
Rhodes, Alexandre de, 10, 11, 18

Ridenhour, Ronald, 128
Russia, *see* Soviet Union

Saigon Military Mission, 37, 39
Salisbury, Harrison, 106–8
School of Law and Administration, Hanoi, 23
Shostakovich, Dmitri, 92–93
Sihanouk, Prince, 77, 78, 80, 134
Society of Foreign Missions, 11–12
South Vietnam, 34–37, 38–43, 98, 99–102, 124, 138
  after U.S withdrawal, 119–22
  army of, *see* ARVN
  beginning of the insurgency against, 44–51
  creation of, 34
  Diem regime, *see* Ngo Dinh Diem
  instability of government of, 66, 75, 99
  Johnson administration's handling of the war, 61–74, 106–8
  Kennedy administration's relations with, 46, 49–51, 54–56, 61–62, 104, 106, 132
  media coverage of the war, 103–9
  Nixon administration's handling of the war, 75–88
  peace negotiations and agreement, 76, 81–88, 108, 119
  Phoenix program, 78

South Vietnam (*cont'd*)
  see also North Vietnam; Vietnam
Soviet Union, 20, 21, 28, 33, 67, 92, 93, 94, 101
Spellman, Cardinal Francis, 36
Stalin, Joseph, 93
Sully, François, 104

Tang dynasty, China, 6
Taylor, Maxwell, 68
Tayson rebellion, 8–9, 12
Tet Offensive, 72–73, 78, 83, 102, 111
Thanh Thai, 23
Thieu Tri, Emperor, 14
Time magazine, 105
Tonkin, 15
Tran Van Tra, 120
Tri Quang, Thich, 53
Trieu Da, 4
Trinh family, 8, 9
Trung Nhi, 6, 7
Trung sisters, 6–7
Trung Trac, 6–7
Tu Duc, 14–15, 16
Tuchman, Barbara, 114

United States, 33, 36, 46
  as colonialist power, 97–98
  debate and opposition to Vietnam War in, 73, 76, 77–78, 80, 82–84, 85–86, 89–115, 140
  Diem regime and, 39, 40, 48, 54–56, 82, 98, 103–4

the doves in, 97–102, 115
  draft dodgers in, 111–14, 141
  effects of Vietnam War on, 131–40
  first Indochina War and, 26–28
  future foreign policy of, 140–42
  the hawks in, 91–96, 99
  Johnson administration, and Vietnam, 61–74, 81, 106–8, 132, 133
  Kennedy administration, and Vietnam, 46, 49–51, 54–56, 61–62, 104, 106, 132
  media coverage of Vietnam War in, 103–9
  Nixon administration, and Vietnam, 75–88, 115, 119, 124, 125, 130, 132, 133
  postwar evaluation of the conflict, 136–140
  veterans of Vietnam War in, 125–30, 136
  Vietnam peace negotiations and agreement, 76, 77, 81–88, 108, 119, 125
U.S. Congress, 63–65, 86, 119, 124, 132, 133
University of the Peoples of the East, 20

Van Ba, *see* Ho Chi Minh
Versailles, Treaty of, 20
Veterans' Medical Care Expansion Act, 130
Veterans of Vietnam War, 125–30, 136–37, 141

Vietcong, *see* National Liberation Front

Vietminh organization, 23, 24, 33, 36–37, 38, 40, 45, 82
   during World War II, 21–23
   founding of, 21, 97
   Indochina War and, 25–30, 33, 38, 98

Vietnam:
   after U.S. withdrawal, 119–24
   early history of, 3–10
   French control of, 14–18
   Geneva accords, 33–37, 43, 44, 49, 98
   Indochina War, 24–30, 38, 95, 98
   nationalists, 18–23, 97
   Western missionaries in, 10–15
   see also North Vietnam; South Vietnam

Vietnam Doc Lap Dong Minh, *see* Vietminh organization

Vietnam War, *see* Indochina War; North Vietnam; South Vietnam; United States

Vietnam War Memorial, 136–37, 141

Vietnamese Special Forces, 54

Vinhyen, 28

Vo Nguyen Giap, 21, 25, 26, 28, 29, 30

Western Europe, 100

Westmoreland, William, 69, 73

Wilson, Woodrow, 20

World Bank, 72

World War I, 20

World War II, 21–22, 67, 130, 131–32

Yale University, 136

Zhou Enlai, 34